DEDICATION

For my mother who excelled in spite of a harsh beginning,
and to my father who never wavered in his love of family.

For Tim and Kristen

For my seven sisters and two brothers who accompanied
me in my finest childhood adventures.

TABLE OF CONTENTS

CHAPTER 1
CHERRY CREEK RIVER

Jennie Duncan covered her mouth with a ragged handkerchief as she walked down Main Street in Cherry Creek River, Colorado. Swirling eddies of fine brown dirt burned her eyes and coated her long eyelashes as she lowered her head looking sideways on her way to the general mercantile. Once inside the musty store, she grumbled to herself as she eyed the long string of boisterous customers waiting in line. The railroad had come to town in 1899. Newcomers were garish and always in too big of a hurry for Jennie Duncan's liking. Even the Arapahos were moving out of their ancient territorial homes to escape the chaos happening in Colorado. In a frantic effort to quell ongoing confrontations between the tribes and settlers, the government took on the task of relocating Indian tribes to other areas. By 1899 the population reached 35,000. The Rocky Mountain gold rush was shifting the focus from ranching and farming to wild and often violent clashes between the miners and tribal members near Central City. Since most of the downtown area was destroyed as a result of fire in 1863, Jennie wanted to leave the Cherry Creek area that bared no resemblance to the familiar place she loved. After her final stop at the mercantile, Jennie shoved her supplies into the wagon in preparation for a trek to Wyoming while there was still land open for homesteading. Tall in stature with strong arms, sky blue eyes, and dense wavy chestnut brown hair added to her strikingly lovely facial features. Her family moved from Pennsylvania farming country to Colorado to homestead when she was young. Jennie's father raised her as if she was the son he longed for. She could hunt, fish and shoot as well or better than any man she knew. She never took no for an answer. Her husband Perry Duncan was also a transplant from Pennsylvania whose family headed west for a new beginning in farming. Moving from the rich dark farming soil in Pennsylvania to the foothills of the Rocky Mountains in Colorado proved to be difficult at best. Perry's childhood was rift with memories of a time when Indian tribes seized upon new settlers, often absconding with food, clothing, weapons and women. As a young man he helped his father and neighboring settlers in Windsor, Colorado build a fort where people in the area would take shelter when various tribes attempted to take back their lands. His family eked out a living in an area near the river where there were often conflicts between the settlers and tribal members. He knew full well how unspeakably brutal those encounters were. Winters were harsh and summers were most often windy, dry and hot. The crops they were accustomed to growing in Pennsylvania did not thrive in the high altitude and dry climate of Colorado. Perry had mixed emotions about leaving Colorado. From sunrise to sundown he worked on the farm to keep the family farm afloat. A tall lanky figure with muscular arms, Perry was known for his quiet temperament. His long curly dark hair and mustache framed his chiseled cheekbones and dark eyes. He was a patient man who did all he could to please his young bride, Jennie; however, there was never any doubt that Jennie called the shots in the Duncan family.

Both Perry's and Jennie's parents died in their fifties after moving to Colorado. Perry's father was killed working on the railroad when a load of railroad ties slipped from a rail car and crushed him. His mother lived only a short time longer and died from consumption. Jennie's father, a farmer and occasional trapper, died after skinning a coyote that had been infested with fleas carrying the bubonic plague. His death came three days after the onset of plague high fever. The sudden death of Jennie's father left the family destitute. Her mother, suddenly widowed, moved back to Pennsylvania with another family who had become disenchanted with Colorado's constant conflicts with Indian tribes and unpredictable Rocky Mountain weather systems. Jennie never saw her mother again after she left Colorado. She learned of her mother's death several months afterwards and harbored a sense of resentment that she had been abandoned on the high plains of Colorado to run the family farm. She continued to operate the farm using the skills her father taught her.

Perry and Jennie met as midlife orphans in their early twenties and married young. Perry was unreservedly in love with Jennie from the first time they met at a livestock auction in Denver where Jennie was selling three of her father's remaining Herefords. After their marriage, they lived on Jennie's family acreage in a log farmhouse warmed by a large rock fireplace and cast iron stove which was brought from Pennsylvania in a covered wagon. The two people Jennie loved most had died in the log home. Her beloved father died in the cabin as well as Jennie's first born infant, Lizzy. She succumbed to small pox in the cabin on a bitter winter evening in December. That night, a night Jennie remembered so well, a brutal wind howled propelling fine snow powder through the chinking of the log cabin where it piled in tiny drifts on the floor and window sills. The joy in Jennie's life seemed to cease with the death of Lizzy. For three months after burying baby Lizzy next to her father in a simple cemetery on the farm, Jennie refused to leave the cabin. Perry took care of the house, the meals, and Jennie during that time. Now, Jennie prepared herself to leave the cabin, leave Colorado, and baby Lizzy behind. Or so she thought.

Three additional children were born to Jennie and Perry since the death of Lizzy: Jessica, Vera and Iris.

Perry appeared to go along with Jennie's impulsive decision to relocate to Sheridan, Wyoming. He secretly alleged that Jennie would come to her senses when she realized how formidable the task of moving the family five hundred miles north through hostile tribal territory would be. Jennie would not be swayed from her decision.

As Jennie carried furniture and cooking utensils to the wagon to load, Perry finally confronted his wife. "Jennie, how can we make this dangerous trip on our own? Let's wait for other families to make the trip and we will have more protection in a group. Please Jennie, can we talk about this?" Jennie spun around to face her husband. "I am making this move, Perry Duncan. You may stay here but I am not staying another day," she bellowed.

As she lifted her children onto the wagon, their long skirts whipped over their heads in the dry Colorado wind.

Behind Jennie's wagon, Perry Duncan pulled another wagon load of furniture, bedding and dried food in burlap sacks. His tattered coat collar was pulled up around his handsome bronzed face while his crumpled, sweat stained hat covered most of it. Only squinted eyes peeked through to daylight.

After the first few miles on the dusty two track trail, the Duncan children were restless. Jennie looked back to give her stern eye look to remind them of her orders to behave. Iris, the youngest, sat beside her while Jessica, the oldest, and Vera, next oldest, sat straight shouldered on the hardwood floor behind. Perry stayed a distance back shrouded in a cloud of choking okra dust left by Jennie's wagon wheels. Words were not spoken except to announce a short stop to water the horses, check the wheels and sip some warm Cherry Creek water from a cow hide canteen.

After several hours on the trail, Jennie watched the dust rising from an approaching wagon. She jerked hard on the reins, reached under her seat to retrieve something wrapped in a burlap bag and placed it under her coat. She turned to the children "I'll do any talking- you best keep quiet." She added loudly "Nobody talks but me- do you understand?" Little heads nodded in unison.

As the approaching wagon got closer Jennie urged her horses faster forward. As the wagons came together she realized the oncoming wagon had stopped. The driver held up his hand to halt Jennie's wagon. Jennie stopped abruptly but said nothing. "There's trouble ahead with a dust storm so bad you can't see the trail" he said. "One of my horses took nearly blind from the dirt". You got about half an hour before the storm gets to you. There's a cottonwood grove along Deer Creek up ahead where you could put up till the storm blows over". The driver tipped his hat and lurched forward. Jennie said nothing. Teeth clenched, she cracked the whip and moved on. Upon arrival at the cottonwood grove protected area, she pushed hard on past it.

Vera blurted out "Ma, the cottonwood grove is there" pointing to the east. "Don't you be telling me nothing, Vera" Don't be sayin' nothin' to nobody". "I do the talking round here". Jesse glanced back to Perry behind and pointed to the cottonwood grove but quickly pulled back when Jennie turned her head.

The sky ahead turned dark yellow and the wind was picking up. Tumbleweeds and sand dust swirled across the trail in murky sheets. Throwing their heads sideways and snorting, the horses blew dust from their nostrils and groaned from the sting. Jennie pulled a handkerchief from beneath the seat to block the dust.

Whimpering, Jesse and Iris covered their faces. Jennie pushed on with no expression, just stiff necked, stern faced horse- whipping silence. Nobody said anything.

As the deep red western sun slipped down over Cheyenne Flats, the prairie sky weaved into a watercolor canvas of orange and pink. The air chilled with a breeze from the northwest as the colors faded and the children in the wagon grew more restless. Everyone needed food. Jennie wanted nothing. Perry wanted to stop the wagon but more than anything, he wanted to see his children's faces and hear their voices.

CHAPTER 2
REPLACING LIZZY

All Jennie could think about was Lizzy. She tried to replace Lizzy three times with these other children. They just never measured up to her precious Lizzy. She fed them and bathed them. There were no lullabies, no bed time stories, and no words of warmth or affection. Those accoutrements were buried with tiny Lizzy in a pine box in Cherry Creek River. Jennie dug up the rose bush she had cut blooms from to place on Lizzy's grave. The rose bush was part of Lizzy she packed with her to travel to Wyoming. The rose bush and all of Lizzy's handmade clothes were all Jennie had left now. Lizzy's clothes could never be left behind. Perry dug up some chokecherry sprigs and an apple sapling from the bottom land near Cherry Creek River. He was leaving everything he knew and loved about Colorado behind. It wasn't his idea to move to Wyoming.

When the prairie skies were too dark to illuminate the trail Jennie brought the wagon to a halt. "Don't just sit there, get yourselves down and gather some rocks for a fire pit if you want some supper" she scowled. Jessica gathered some of the heaviest rocks near the side of the trail while the younger ones carried what they could handle. Perry pulled his wagon closer to Jennie's wagon but didn't approach Jennie or the children. He pulled a hay bale from the wagon to feed the horses and brought a pile of hay to Jennie's horses, never lifting his eyes to her face. He silently returned to his wagon and swung the hay bale back on to the rig. Silently he prepared his bedroll for the night.

Jennie started a fire using dried grass and crushed sagebrush branches near the trail. The aroma of the burning sage hung over the campsite in an eerie pungent fog. . The air, cold now, stilled with the sunset. Jennie's children sat around the fire on the rocks they gathered. Jessica carried a tin plate of dried beef jerky and broth to "the old man", the name Jennie used scornfully. When Jessica returned Jennie said "I'm putting this fire out before the snakes come in to warm themselves. Get yourselves in the wagon and into your bedrolls while there's some light. We'll be starting out at daybreak".

Perry's wagon creaked like an old rocking chair as he climbed up to bed down on the seat. The Arapahos at Cherry Creek River taught the white man not to sleep on the prairie floor. Rattlers swarmed to bedrolls seeking heat. Jennie, wrapped in a sheepskin hide, stayed up most of the night staring into the prairie darkness. She yearned for Lizzy to be resting in her arms instead of rotting in the pine box in Cherry Creek River.

Without chirping birds, daybreak crept over the horizon. The sepia treeless prairie offered little beyond a brief pale strip of pink sunrise to receive the new day. Occasionally a wayward meadowlark or magpie fluttered by on the way to a better place.

Crushing dried sage leaves in her hands, Jenny stacked the leaves to start a small fire. She boiled water for a half cup of coffee.

Perry had risen before her and started feeding the horses before sunrise. By the time the children woke the horses were rigged up for the day's trip north to Cheyenne, Wyoming. Jennie planned for a stop there to get supplies for the long trip to Sheridan. She heard there was a mercantile near the new train depot in Cheyenne.

Before breakfast Jennie's children ventured out to explore some of the rock outcroppings in the early morning. Pockets were stuffed with sparkly rock chips. Jessica found a five point rattle left from a snake that had nested near the rocks. Jennie looked toward the children without speaking. Noticing her glance, they knew it time to return to the wagon. They knew the look. They knew it was time to be quiet.

Rain hadn't fallen in weeks. The gray powder dirt that coated Jennie's face gave her the look of being beyond her years. As her wagon moved forward, her face held no expression. She was getting farther away from Lizzy in Cherry Creek River. She kept thinking of her best born child being left behind. Perry could do nothing to console her anymore. He quit trying. She blamed him somehow. He never asked why. Small Pox wasn't his doing.

CHAPTER 3
CHEYENNE

Log cabins dotted the ridges on the horizon. Less traveled dirt trails veered off from the main trail and disappeared over naked sagebrush hills. Ahead, clouds of dust rose and hung over the prairie floor like a dirty blanket. Jennie's children perked with interest at the sights ahead. The rutted dirt streets were busy with tall hatted men and women in long skirts. Barking dogs chased after Jennie's wagon as if they knew she didn't belong there. As the wagon creaked to a stop in Cheyenne, Jennie turned to the children "Nobody says nothing to nobody. I'll do the talking. You wait in the wagon for me. Do you understand?" Little heads nodded again.

The mercantile, a tall two story building built from weathered gray milled lumber, was the main attraction on the busy Main Street. Next to the mercantile, a saloon called "Flats" shared a common wall. Noise from the rowdy saloon drifted through the walls and into the street as Jennie passed by. She pulled her wagon to the side of the building and jumped off with a glance back, then disappeared around the corner. Perry lingered behind only to get off his wagon and check the horses. He approached Jennie's wagon and did the same assessment. Looking up at the children, he smiled and winked. Twisting their necks, they watched him return to his wagon.

A scruffy bearded man in heavy weathered chaps strolled by Jennie's wagon, stopped and looked up at the three young ones. Jennie, carrying a wooden box of supplies, appeared around the corner at the same time. Tipping his hat, the stranger said, "That's a fine group of young ladies you have here". He looked up at Jessica and said "What's your name, little lady?" Jessica, gasping panic-stricken, looked at Jennie. "Jennie blurted out "We don't have time for conversation, sir". "Can I give you a hand Ma'am?" He said. "No sir, you cannot," she snapped. Tipping his hat again, he walked away glancing back at Jennie and the children. Perry, watching from his wagon seat behind, dropped his head.

Without a word, Jennie grasped her long dusty skirt and pulled herself back up on the rig.

Vera warily asked "Ma, can we get down for a spell?" "We got no more business here", she said, then whipped the reins so hard the wagon lunged forward sending the children tipping backward off their seats.

Looking back, Vera watched Perry jump off his wagon and slowly walk around the corner to the mercantile. Vera spoke in a half whisper "Pa isn't behind us Ma." Jennie didn't respond. It was more of that horse-whipping silence.

CHAPTER 4

STORMY

Jennie's wagon was a good quarter mile ahead of Perry's. Vera and Jessica kept peering back around the canvas side of the wagon to see if their father was in sight yet. Jennie never looked back once. A man in the Cheyenne Mercantile told her that the Lakota Sioux and Northern Cheyenne Indians were "on the fight" in northern Wyoming and maybe she should wait to travel with more wagons headed that way. Jennie didn't much care about waiting. "No stranger was going to steer my wagon", she muttered to herself. In her mind, the next stop would be on the banks of the Laramie River near Wheatland. The trail out of Cheyenne heading north was flat and smooth. She would make good time if she kept whipping those horses. The Laramie River was too far to reach that day no matter how hard she whipped. Daylight was vanishing fast. Gloom dropped over the prairie. Steering her wagon sharply off the trail, she rough halted her horses.

A black speck on the horizon, Perry's wagon appeared behind. The children spied their father's wagon approaching and jumped waving their arms and shrieking. "Stop this right now!" Jennie scorned. Voices carried on the prairie. Jennie feared who else or what else may become aware of the commotion. With darkness setting in, there was work to be done. She sensed that she driven the wagon too long and left little time for night preparations. Lightening to the west could bring rain to the prairie or possibly wind or fire.

Jennie murmured to herself as she watched the children running on the dusky evening prairie. Vera's long wispy curls bounced with every jump. She felt a pang of nausea as she sat motionless. She did miss having Perry at her side. Their heated argument before leaving Colorado still churned inside her gut. Perry questioned their move to Sheridan again. Jennie remembered how she lashed out in anger toward him. She wanted to leave the memory of Lizzy's death in Colorado. She now realized that it was migrating with her, hanging around her neck like a cold stone.

The sky was near dark now except for the explosive lightening which lit the clouds like a giant flash bulb to the southwest. A deep muffled rumble of thunder filled the air amid the children's laughter far from the wagon. Jennie listened as Perry's wagon creaked to a halt behind hers. Approaching Jennie for the first time since they left Cherry Creek, he said, "Jennie, let me help you rig up for the night. Let the children run till the storm gets closer." Jennie looked into Perry's eyes then quickly looked to the ground and nodded. "I could use some help tonight". She turned away, and then briefly glanced back at Perry as he busied himself with the horses. Maybe, just maybe things will be better in Wyoming, she thought.

Vera and Jessica burst into camp breathless. Shrieking, they pointed to the sky to the south. Perry and Jennie looked just as the lemon yellow lightening lit enough to see a white funnel snaking from the sky to the ground. When the horses began snorting and pulling back from the hackles, Perry scooped Vera and Iris from the ground. With a child under each arm and Jessica in tow, he stumbled in the shadows to a rock outcropping and left the children there. Unaware that Perry had gotten the children to protection of the rocks, Jennie frantically thrashed through the sagebrush shrieking Jessica's name. Perry's eyes combed the shadowy camp area to catch a glimpse of Jennie's body. Her silhouette flashed into view with the next intense streak of lightening. He could hear the sound of Jennie's long skirt flapping in the wind like a tall ship sail, but had to wait till the next flash of light to see which direction to run. Crumpled on the ground like a discarded rag doll, Jennie had covered her head. Perry dove on top of her to shield her from the wicked barrage of wind driven sand and hail. Jennie's shrieks were muffled under the weight of Perry's body. Amidst the sound of roaring winds, the wagons creaked and groaned in the surging winds. Far off clanking of metal cooking pots sounded almost musical as they tumbled across the prairie floor. As quickly as the violence began, it ended in a hush. Perry lifted himself from Jennie. She grasped his arm and whispered "the children, we need to find them". Still clenching his arm, her face lingered in the heavy fabric of his jacket. Motionless in a heap, they listened to the faint cries of their children drifting through the darkness like voices from a far-away church choir.

CHAPTER 5

AFTER THE STORM

Nothing remained in the place it was before the storm. The ferocious storm cloud had traveled quickly to the east but the accompanying lightening still lit the prairie from a distance. Inching their way over the hail covered ground back to Jennie and Perry, the traumatized children clung to their parents as they were checked for injuries. Gone to the prairie silence, the horses were nowhere to be found. Perry managed to light a fire from a stack of tumbleweeds that gathered next to Jennie's twisted wagon. His wagon was toppled and had turned facing a different direction. From the dim light of the fire, they could see that Jennie's wagon was leaning. One of the wheels had twisted. Attempting to bring some normalcy to the situation, Perry brought dried beef strips and bread from his wagon. The family ate their meager meal seated on the soggy dirt floor of the prairie.

Rummaging in the dark to retrieve bedding from Jennie's wagon, Perry handed each child a blanket, instructing them to go to Jennie's wagon and bed down. "Make do with what you have and we will put it all back together in the morning", he said in a hushed voice. Jessica, Vera and Iris carried their blankets to the leaning wagon, perched their feet on the step and jumped into the back under the cover of the canvas walls. Sleep came quickly for them this night in spite of the calamity of the night.

Perry and Jennie spent some time gathering what they could see strewn around the camp. Jennie crawled on her knees, pawing the ground for her gun. She hoped that morning would reveal the circumstances of the gun.

Brushing the hail stones aside, Perry arranged wool blankets on the ground near the overturned wagon. He motioned to Jennie to join him on the prairie floor. " I'll keep the snakes away, Jennie." Without comment, she laid with Perry. The sky, now clear and star speckled, showed no sign of restlessness. Neither did Jennie or Perry. They hadn't slept together for longer than either could remember. This night they longed for each other's warmth.

Dawn peeked over the horizon like light showing through a half-pulled window shade. Perry was up and moving about without a sound. Before starting any other task, he knew that the horses needed to be located and brought back to camp. Surely they couldn't have gone too far since the prairie offered little food. Perry worried that they might be seeking water. He understood this would prove disastrous if the horses found suitable surroundings and did not choose to return to camp. Perry's horses were not pets, but working livestock. He walked to a high ridge to search for signs of the horses but couldn't see far enough in the early light. When the sun got higher in the sky he would have a better chance at seeing them on the horizon. If any Indian tribesmen caught sight of them, he knew he would never see his horses again. Well trained horses were more valuable than gold nuggets to the Indians.

Distracted by this failure to locate the horses, he meandered toward camp and set about gathering items from a quarter mile away that had blown towards the northwest. He came upon Jennie's empty rose bush pot. Picking up the pot, he stared into it. Glancing back toward the wagon where Jennie laid buried under the mountain of blankets, he suddenly felt the pain again of the loss of his daughter Lizzy. He couldn't let Jennie see the empty flower pot.

As daylight grew stronger in the east, Perry saw the glistening metal cooking pots scattered amidst the sagebrush. Since the wagon trail essentially traveled northwest from their current location, he hoped he might find lost items as they got moving again. The question was, when could they get moving again? The prospect of getting Jennie's wagon back up was not good with a disabled wheel and he knew they weren't going anywhere without the horses. Kicking the white dirt under his feet, he stomped in frustration. This turn of events was not how the move to Wyoming was supposed to happen. When he turned to head back to the wagon, he caught sight of Jennie's shiny green leafed rose bush lodged in the branches of tall withered sagebrush. He rushed to retrieve the bare root rose bush.

Kneeling on the ground, he scratched at the hard sandy prairie dirt with his weathered hands till he managed to gather enough powdery soil to cover the roots of the rose bush in the pot. How could this rose bush survive the trauma of the storm? Could it thrive in the lifeless replenished sandy prairie soil after living in the rich dark Cherry Creek soil it was planted in? Perry had more solemn tasks to consider at this point but he knew that Jennie's heart would be broken if the rose bush didn't make it to Sheridan. She couldn't bring Lizzy, but she could bring Lizzy's roses.

The brighter morning light revealed the true extent of the turmoil left from the storm. Perry questioned in his mind once again the move to Wyoming. Life in Cherry Creek had its order. There was no order here today. Jennie's life was without order for so long that Perry knew Jennie wouldn't recognize this situation as perilous. She measured every event in comparison to losing Lizzy. No event, no chaos or catastrophe even came close to the tragedy of finding her little Lizzy's body lifeless and cold. In the defining moment of Lizzy's death, Jennie's life instantly distorted into periods of irrational comparisons. Perry had now come to fear that Jennie led the family into this perilous situation without considering the possible consequences of traveling alone in primitive tribal territory. He knew better. He only wanted to make a new life for Jennie and if this was what she needed, he would do this for her. How foolish could he have been? He let his heart rule over his head this time. Jennie had a way of doing that to him.

CHAPTER 6

RATTLESNAKE REVENGE

Quivering his shoulders in melancholy, Perry decided that this was no time for regrets and second guessing. He had to devise a plan to get his family to some sort of safe haven. Holding Jennie in his arms last night brought back a sense of engagement with her. Today he didn't feel the lonely detachment as if he was just a player in some obscure melodrama. He had grave concerns about their situation but now felt a new sense of commitment to find a way to get his family to Sheridan, Wyoming. This wasn't the time to turn back to Colorado. There was nothing there for him. Jennie needed to find a new place, a new peace.

The horses must be found. The wagon must be repaired.

Off in the distance, in the morning light, Perry saw a faint wisp of dust rising from the ground. He ran to a rise to get a better view of the source of the dust cloud. He was able to make out the silhouette of a horse, then another, and then he could see that one of the horses had a rider. A cold chill ran through him. It tingled to his gritty scalp. Memories of brutal Indian attacks near Windsor, Colorado brushed across his mind. Was this trouble galloping toward the crippled wagon and his family? There is no place to hide on the prairie. Where can he send his children to safety? Running faster than the oncoming horses, he reached the wagon and yelled, "Get up!" Little heads jerked up from under blankets and Jennie shocked awake. Perry whispered to Jennie to take the children and hide in the tallest sagebrush they could find till he called to them to return. Jennie's skirt twirled around in a graceful pirouette as her eyes frantically searched again for her burlap wrapped weapon. There was no time to find that gun now. She swept her barefoot little ones up and disappeared over a shallow ridge. Their only chance to be hidden was to lay face-down flat on the prickly prairie floor.

Perry's heart thumped harder as the horses and rider drew closer. He could feel thick hot blood coursing through the veins in his head. The early intense sun burned his eyes as he tried to focus on the oncoming cloud. Rushing to the wagon, he retrieved one of his rifles from the wagon box. How many were there now? Was there more than one rider? Why were they coming toward the camp with such speed? Were Jennie and the children going to be safe? The sound of the pounding hooves thundered now. Perry took cover behind the overturned wagon and searched the prairie horizon behind him for his wife and children. Jennie, he knew, would do what was necessary.

She was strong and capable.

The shroud of horses slowed as they approached camp now. Perry poised himself for confrontation. He peeked around the corner of the side board and took a one eyed look at the horses and rider. A bearded man peered back. Perry pondered whether this was trouble. The sound of snorting horses, swishing tails and heavy horse breathing was loud now. Then a coarse roaring voice broke through. "Man, are these your horses?" At that moment Perry realized he didn't even question whether the horses were his. He slowly moved from behind the wagon with his gun still pointing at the stranger. "Man, you best put down your weapon. There's no fight here", the stranger yelled. Perry took a deep breath. Exhaling, his shoulders drooped and his gun lowered. "Yes, those are two of my horses. I have two more missing". The stranger dismounted his horse slowly and stepped closer to Perry. "Looks like you had some trouble in the storm last night, Mister". "Do you have a spare wheel for that wagon?" Perry kicked the dirt. "Hell no, and I got a wife and three young ones to get to Sheridan before the food runs out". The stranger stretched out his heavy gloved hand to Perry. "Augustine is my name, what's yours?" "Duncan, Perry Duncan" he said. "Where you coming from, Duncan?" Perry hesitated, almost dreading to murmur the words, "Cherry Creek".

Augustine looked around the campsite chaos and said "I'll help you right up your good wagon but not much I can help with the other without a spare wheel or tools to make a repair". Perry stared out to the horizon and said the wagon wasn't much good without the other two horses anyway. Augustine added that there was a band of Indians in the area who would probably find and keep the horses. "You got a place near here?" Perry asked in a hushed tone. "My wife is hell bent on making it to Sheridan but I am running out of hope to make that happen". Augustine scanned the prairie horizon in search of Perry's family. "I got a small place near Middle Bear if you want to put up for a day or two but I don't have a wheel that would work for that wagon. I could use a hand with some fencing and I'll pay some to help you get supplies for the rest of the trip", he said. Jennie's disheveled head of chestnut brown hair popped up from behind a rock just long enough to see if there was anything happening with the stranger who rode into camp. She was far enough away that she couldn't hear the conversation.

She saw that Perry and the stranger were standing close to each other and neither one had a gun drawn. Next to her, Vera stirred. Jennie pushed Vera's head to the ground. "No, stay down till Pa comes to get us", she said. Jessica and Iris covered their heads with their tiny dirty hands. They were rarely in the company of strangers and when they were, they were to remain silent.

Shuffling his battered leather boots through the sagebrush toward his family, Perry called out to Jennie. Standing up, Jennie cautiously joined Perry and the stranger. The little ones stayed hidden, heads covered. Perry introduced Jennie to Augustine who tipped his hat to her. "Mam" was all he said. Perry told Jennie that they would follow Augustine to his place on Middle Bear to stay just long enough to get the wagon repaired. Frowning, she pushed hair back from her face. She knew she had no control over the plan. Perry told her that they would have to put all their remaining supplies into one wagon to get to Middle Bear.

Augustine and Perry took to the task of righting the toppled wagon. After a few attempts, it became apparent that the two of them couldn't move the heavy wagon without Jennie's help. Jennie was strong. Her arms were lean and muscular. Perry and Augustine pushed up on the ends and Jennie grasped the heavy wooden beam at the middle of the wagon. Once the wagon had tipped up, there was no stopping the downward motion and it crashed onto the wheels jarring the supplies inside. A cotton bag of flour had split open puffing a white cloud out the end of the wagon like steam from a train engine. Perry motioned to Jennie. "Gather the children", he said. Jennie started walking to the rock outcropping seeing the children's little heads peeking above the sandstone. She mustered half a smile at the sight. How she longed to see the blue eyes and curly blonde hair of her sweet Lizzy there with the others.

Just as Jennie reached the rock outcropping, Jessica shrieked. Jennie eyes filled with terror as she watched a fat diamond back rattlesnake slither away from the rock across the hard packed prairie floor. Jessica was clutching her arm still crying in a shrill bizarre tone. Perry and Augustine jerked around to the commotion. Jennie, now breathless spoke to Jessica in a soft whisper. "Don't move now, lay down here while I get Pa". She jolted around to call to Perry and found him standing over her wild eyed. "It's a snake bite Pa.", she whispered. Perry dug into his pocket and pulled out a knife and in an instant had pierced his child's arm from fang mark to fang mark. He covered the slash with his mouth and sucked blood and venom from the wound. Jessica, now pale faced and blue mouthed, lay limp on the ground gasping for air in terror. Jennie's trembling hand stroked her child's forehead. The stranger Augustine spoke abruptly. "Let me take the child to my place now". My wife has a tincture given to her by an Indian woman for snake bites. You need to trust me with this, folks". Jennie and Perry looked into each other's eyes, both searching for the answer. Perry nodded and gathered Jessica in his arms. The child was cradled on the saddle in front of Augustine's lap as he whipped the horse ahead. Jennie crumpled to the ground as the horse hooves left a cloud of white prairie dust swirling in the air.

CHAPTER 7

THE LOST TRAIL

Perry stood speechless watching the stranger gallop away with his child. He pointed to one of the horses brought back by Augustine and told Jennie to follow behind them. "The child needs you to be there. Take the horse and we'll bring the wagon". Perry lifted Jennie to the back of the horse. Her hair flew wildly in the air as she rode away slapping the horse's rump.

Squinting in the morning glare, the dry wind burned her eyes. She had lost sight of Augustine and Jessica's horse. She followed the hoof tracks as best she could until she realized that she could no longer distinguish any tracks. The treeless prairie horizon left her disoriented. Panic settled into her bones. Somehow she had veered off the trail. She drew the horse to a stop and closed her eyes to calm herself. "This can't be happening" she whispered. Perched on the horse's back, she turned in every direction looking for some sign of movement. None was to be found. She knew the sun was in the east but she and Perry never asked the stranger with their child where his home was. She was alone on that parched flat prairie. Sliding off the horse, she rested her head on his soft side. She needed to pull her thoughts together. At that instant a bird fluttered from a stand of sagebrush nearby and the horse leapt forward. Jennie jumped and grabbed for the reins, sending the horse into a full gallop off across the prairie. "He'll come back", she thought. He has to come back. She fell to her knees. Kneeling on the ground, Jennie felt her heart sink. Alone in this strange place, she believed her dream of going to Sheridan was slipping away. Her only hope was that Perry would find her. What if he didn't even look for her? How could she blame him? Day after day, she merely went about with chores and childcare. Perry didn't have any of her heart anymore. She buried that broken heart with her Lizzy and it really didn't matter to her anymore.

The sun was high overhead now. It must be noon, Jennie thought. There was no breeze to indicate which direction she should walk. She knew that the prevailing winds usually came from the northwest, but in Wyoming the wind could come from the southeast as well. She was still too far south to see Casper Mountain and too far north now to see the Rocky Mountains above Cherry Creek River. She could see a faint silhouette of a mountain to her left but she didn't know if Augustine's homestead was east or west. The mountains always provided a sense of direction to Jennie. Without them, she was lost. Now she was misplaced. Perry, Vera and Iris were misplaced as well, misplaced out in the middle of nowhere. Stranger Augustine was Jessica's best hope now. She decided to walk in the direction of the faint mountain. She couldn't stay in the place where she was. Her lips were dry from the hot air and dust. There wasn't a green tree in sight which might indicate a water source.

CHAPTER 8
WATER FOR JENNIE

Jennie needed to find the trail. How could she have gotten so far from the trail?

Because the terrain was so flat, there was no way to locate the trail. If she could get to higher ground it might be possible to peruse the prairie floor. Just ahead she thought there was a small rise. Her pace quickened to reach the rise in the ground. She reached the summit of the small swell. Standing tall, she looked in every direction but found no trail markings. Something caught her eye as she looked into the distance. There was movement. Something was moving quickly enough to create dust cloud. Standing motionless like a statue, Jennie felt a rush of hope move through her body. Maybe it was Perry and the children. Perhaps it was her horse returning to her. Still motionless, Jennie had another thought. What if the approaching movement was not Perry? The man at the mercantile in Cheyenne warned that there was a band of Indians causing trouble ahead. She slowly crouched to her knees glaring at the oncoming dust cloud. It was like whatever or whoever she was seeing was coming directly toward her. Maybe she should hide until she recognized who was coming her way.

Jennie slowly crawled off the top of the rise and slid behind a large mound of sage brush. Lying flat on the ground now, she peeked through the prickly branches. She could make out more than one figure now. Swallowing hard, she thought "This could be good, or this could be bad", The realization hit her hard now. It wasn't Perry. Now she could see there were four figures coming fast on horses. Jennie froze. Every muscle in her tired body tightened. Eyes widened, she could see that the four riders were Indians. She held her breath so long that she felt dizzy. It felt like a white misty curtain was dropping over her eyes. The horses and riders abruptly stopped, craning their necks. Scanning the area, one of them seemed to be focused on Jennie's sagebrush blind and inched his horse a few steps closer to her. She noticed that the horse had had three red feathers woven into its mane. She could feel her heart pounding the ground beneath her breast. If they came any closer they would surely see her. If they rode anywhere around her they were bound to catch sight of her dusty figure. Without a word, the riders turned their horses. The youngest looking rider with the red feathered horse mane, glanced back over his shoulder. Jennie felt his eyes meet hers through the pale green branches. "He saw me", she whispered. Now she was breathing hard as if she was re-gaining all the breaths she held inside for those long minutes. Still motionless, she watched the riders move farther away from her. She saw something drop to the ground from the young man who glanced back at her once again. She believed that whatever was dropped was meant for her. When the riders were no longer vis-ible, she slowly rose from the ground to her wobbly knees. She tasted the pungent sage she had been nestled in. Crouching, she made her way to the area where something fell from the rider. Crumpled on the ground she found a drawstring leather pouch half full of warm water. She sniffed the liquid. It was water. Why did this young Indian leave this water for her? Was he planning to return to gather her for himself? Jennie had no inclination to speculate. She was thirsty and hungry. She sipped the water to wet her parched lips. Her muscles ached. Now she had the hoof prints of the horses to follow. Where would they lead her? Squeezing the leather pouch in her trembling hand, she chose to follow the riders.

CHAPTER 9

A LOST WAY

The sun lowered in the sky. Back at camp, Perry and the children had loaded their supplies into the remaining wagon. As the wagon swayed and creaked along the rutted trail toward Augustine's homestead, Perry assured the children they would meet up with Ma and Jessica soon, even though he knew his children were too young to understand that their snake bit sibling could have died before reaching Augustine's homestead. He tried to engage the two youngsters in conversation. They were silent young passengers. Jennie did the talking for them back in Cherry Creek River. They were listeners, mostly.

Perry knew his that children understood on some unspoken level that their mother was still grieving the loss of their older sister in Cherry Creek River. Lizzy was always first in Jennie's heart. She dressed all her children in dead Lizzy's clothes. At times they protested. Jennie ignored the protests. Perry could not intervene for his children anymore in the clothes discussion. He tried to step in and was firmly defeated. All of Lizzy's clothes were lovingly and meticulously sewn by Jennie. Some of the dresses were never worn by Lizzy since Jennie made dresses for Lizzy well in advance of her need for them. Jennie braided Jessica, Iris and Vera's long hair in precisely the same way she braided Lizzy's. Perry understood that this was Jennie's way of keeping Lizzy with her.

As the sun sank deeper into the horizon, Perry had driven his wagon in the direction Augustine had described to him. He identified two buildings to the west of the trail and knew these buildings must be Augustine's homestead. He pushed the horses faster as he approached the turn off trail to the buildings. Imagining seeing his Jennie and Jessica warm inside the home of the stranger, gave him comfort. The sunset turned pale orange over the log buildings. Perry wanted more than anything to bring his family back together under the brilliant coral sky.

Bringing the wagon to a halt, he jumped off his wagon holding his hand up to the children to stay. Augustine opened the door to his home and called to Perry to bring the others inside. Perry returned to the wagon and hurriedly gathered the children to the ground. Searching Augustine's eyes for answers, Perry quickened his pace. Augustine flung the heavy door open wide to reveal little Jessica lying on a cot. Jessica started to jump up when Perry's face appeared in the doorway, but dropped back to the cot. Jessica smiled. Perry searched the room for Jennie. "Where is my wife?" he asked. Augustine, with a puzzled look, answered "Your wife is not here", Just then Augustine's wife entered the room from the back room. She went to Jessica's cot and put her hand on Jessica's forehead. "This little one is doing fine now, sir", she said in a light hearted voice. Perry and Augustine stood motionless. Augustine looked vacantly toward Perry and said, "This is my wife Catherine". Perry responded, "Nice to meet you, Catherine". "My wife Jennie was supposed to meet us here. She left camp hours ago to follow Augustine". The room thickened with silence. Perry jerked around to the door. Augustine followed him and yelled "It is too dark, man. You won't be able to find your wife at this hour!"

Stopping dead in this tracks, Perry looked back at Augustine. His eyes were panic wide. "My God, what could have happened to her?" Augustine responded "Come inside. My wife has prepared some food. You need to eat something. We will go out at first light". We will find your wife". Brushing his long hair from his face, Perry followed Augustine into the house. Jessica was now sitting up with bandaged arm and puffy flushed cheeks. Vera and Iris stood silently at Jessica's side. Catherine told Perry that she tried to give Jessica a warm bath but Jessica refused. "I think she will feel even better to get some of the prairie dust from her hair and clothes" she said softly. "I can prepare a bath for all three of the girls if you wish", Catherine added. Perry looked at Catherine and covered his face with his calloused hands. "Thank you, Catherine, can we just get some rest now? We are all tired and hungry". Catherine nodded. "Of course, the baths can wait".

In the warmth of the cabin, beef soup and homemade bread was a meal the Duncan family ate with fervor. Even little Jessica ate for the first time since the snake bite incident. Catherine sat at Jessica's side hand spooning the soup to the child whose tiny lips were cracked and red from fever. "We'll have your Ma here soon", she said looking around the table to the children.

Perry rushed through his meal. Still bewildered by Jennie's absence, he asked Augustine if there was any other homesteads nearby that Jennie could have mistaken for Augustine and Catherine's. Augustine looked at Perry guardedly telling him there wasn't another homestead for miles. "What about Indians?" Perry asked. Catherine and Augustine glanced at each other, each hoping the other would answer Perry's question. Augustine finally answered "We have heard there are three or four Crow Indians scouting around from up near Montana". Nobody has much information and there is no talk of trouble but we don't hear too much unless we get to Casper to pick up supplies". Perry wasn't familiar with the Crow Tribe since the Arapahos were prominent in Cherry Creek River. He felt comfortable with the Arapahos since they had come to terms with the white man in Colorado, as long as there was no provocation.

"Jennie's a strong woman", Perry announced loudly, looking around the table. "She will find her way back to us one way or another". Augustine, glancing at the children said, "If she doesn't find us first, we will find her first. Now, Catherine, where is that gooseberry pie you made for our guests?" Jumping up from her chair, Catherine flashed a smile back to Augustine. "As soon as we find your wife we need to load up some tools and get your other wagon back up" Augustine said in attempt to give Perry and the children something else to think about. Perry was staring out the window into the darkness. He heard none of the goings on around the table. He pondered how Jennie took no food or water with her as she galloped away from camp to follow Augustine and snake- bit Jessica. He quietly recounted his last sight of Jennie as she bolted away from camp on the horse.

Catherine carried the warm gooseberry pie to the table. Jessica's eyes were wide with enchantment. Iris and Vera perked up in their chairs. "Gooseberries are about all we find around here in the fall, and we have to get to the berries before the birds do" Catherine whispered.

CHAPTER 10
A NIGHT IN MIDDLE BEAR

Now alone, darkness had swallowed Jennie. In Cherry Creek River she could always look around and see lights dotting the horizon even on the darkest of nights. The Wyoming prairie offered only silence and sporadic breezes that swooshed through the sage. She walked until she could no longer make out the horse hoof prints in the dirt. Kneeling down, she brushed away the prickly dry grass and sat with her arms squeezing her knees together. The sky was clear. The moon, a pale sliver of white in the east, hung above. Curling up, she lay on the hard ground and covered her face with her long skirt. Her gray cotton petticoat was crispy white when she left Colorado. It secluded her weary scratched legs from the cold, dark night air.

Wrestling with her clothing throughout the night, Jennie tried to warm her body against the cold night breezes. When the first tinge of dawn appeared on the horizon, she allowed herself to fall into a deep sleep. She woke with a start jumping to her knees upright. She felt a presence near her and jerked around to see a man standing behind her holding his hand up as if to calm her frenzied face. Falling backwards, she was now in a sitting position looking up into the face of a young Indian man. She vaguely recognized him as perhaps the one who left her the water pouch. Her thought came, "he did come back for me". The young man remained still. His face was calm. Paralyzed with fear, she sat motionless searching his face for intent. Rising slowly to standing position, she looked around her for any kind of clue as to her fate. He was alone. The silence between them had to break. Jennie lifted her chin up and said "why are you here?" The young man replied to her "I come to give food. I come to help you". "But, why?" she whispered. He gave no answer. Reaching into his soft leather tunic, he brought out some dried meat and flat bread wrapped in leather much like the water pouch he left for Jennie. Staying at a safe distance, he stretched out his hand to Jennie. She searched his face again and took a step closer to the man. Her hands slowly opened to accept the food, and then quickly stepped backwards again.

"My mother was helped by white woman", he said with his face looking down. "White woman helped my mother in sickness". "Now, I help white woman to honor my mother". Jennie took a bite of the bread offered by the man. She felt panic leaving her chest. "Help me to find my family", she said. "They are at a homestead near here with my sick child who was bitten by a snake". The young Indian's eyes widened. "My mother give snake medicine to white woman!" he said in excitement. Jennie's face softened as looked at the young man. "Can you take me to the home of the white woman?" "I will show you trail to white woman house", he said in a hushed tone. The young Indian clapped his hand once and clicked his tongue loudly. A lofty buckskin horse with red feathers in the mane came running toward them from behind Jennie. She was surprised she hadn't seen or heard the animal. "You ride horse", the young man said. He motioned for Jennie to mount the horse. She grabbed the soft mane and hurled herself on to the back of the horse. The young man silently walked ahead of the horse. No words were spoken between Jennie and this young Indian man as she perused the horizon for any sign of a homestead. Hours passed as she silently rode behind the young man. The sun, high overhead now, signaled mid-day. The young man held up his hand and the horse stopped dead in his tracks. Motioning for Jennie to come down from the horse, he stepped aside while Jennie slid off the horse. Searching the man's face for some clue why he made her come off the horse, Jennie poised to take flight. He pointed to a tree branch fence post ahead and told Jennie to follow the tree branch posts to the white woman's home. "You see house over hill", he said. Jennie took a step closer to the man. He stepped backward. "Go", he said. Jennie started walking in the direction of the tree branch post and turned around to see the young man standing next to his horse. He raised his hand to her then mounted his horse and fled. Grabbing at her long flapping skirt, she ran in the direction of the next post. Post after post flew past her as she ran. She couldn't remember when she had run so fast and long. She stopped to catch her breath as she reached the next old branch post. Jennie glanced back to see if the young Indian man was still in view. He had disappeared. At that moment she heard yelling in the distance. Someone was calling but she could not make out the direction of the sound. Seemingly out of nowhere, Jennie saw Perry on his horse with arms waving wildly in the air as he rode toward her. He jumped from his horse while the animal still hurtled forward. "Jennie!" He heaped her into his arms. Her pale face, buried in his chest, crumpled in tears. "My God, woman, I have found you", he whispered into her tangled hair. "Jessica", how is Jessica?" Jennie mustered the question in a raw voice. Clutching her tightly, looking into Jennie's face, Perry said "Jessica is fine." 'We are all fine now", Perry closed his eyes as he pulled Jennie to his chest again.

Lifting Jennie to the horse, Perry flung himself up behind her. With one arm wrapped tightly around her waist, he nudged the horse ahead. Leaning back, Jennie rested her head against Perry as they rode. She had not ridden with Perry like this since before Lizzy was born. Her heart softened as the horse's rhythm moved them steadily forward. Her body relaxed as she felt Perry's breath warm and moist on the back of her neck.

CHAPTER 11

REUNION AT MIDDLE BEAR

Augustine and Catherine's home came into view just beyond a stand of small cottonwood trees. Jennie hadn't seen green grass since they left Cheyenne. As they drew closer to the house, she could see the little ones and a woman standing by the front door waving. Jessica stood with the others by the door to greet Jennie. With the little arm still bandaged, Jessica was waving with the others. Jumping off the horse, Perry turned to help Jennie only to find that she had leapt down on her own and was already making her way to the children. Wiggling arms wrapped around her legs while she stooped to Jessica's eye level. "My little child", Jennie said tearfully. Jessica pointed to Catherine and said "Catherine took care of me, Ma". Jennie stood up. Walking to Catherine she offered her hand to this woman who saved her child's life. Catherine pulled Jennie in and hugged her heartily. Jennie looked into Catherine's face and knew that this was the woman who ultimately may have saved her life as well since she was the woman who had saved the young Indian man's mother. Jennie held this information close to her heart for the time. Around the side of the log house came Augustine with a wide grin on his weathered face. "Well, isn't this a sight to see?" he yelled with both arms in the air.

Jennie's eyes examined her children. Their skirts and cotton blouses had been laundered. Their long curls were shiny clean. They looked as if they just left Cherry Creek. Catherine watched Jennie's face as the realization hit her that her children had been fed, bathed and tenderly cared for in Jennie's absence. Jennie's eyes flashed at Catherine briefly. Her children had never been away from her for even a day. Nobody had ever tended to their needs except Jennie. Catherine, never taking her eyes off Jennie, said "these children are the most well behaved children I have ever been around". Jennie bowed her head and said "thank you, Catherine". Watching from a wooden chair by the fireplace, Perry jumped to his feet. "Jennie is a good mother". We lost a child in Colorado. Our first child, Lizzy died in a Small Pox outbreak. Jennie is still coping with our loss." Catherine closed her eyes. "I am so sorry for your loss Jennie and Perry", she said.

"Can we go outside? Vera asked timidly. Jennie nodded, staring blankly at Catherine. The door flung open and the children hurried outside. Little Jessica hobbled behind the others.

Catherine moved into the kitchen and busied herself with preparing some soup. The aroma of fresh baked bread wafted through the room. "Jennie, surely you would like to freshen up some too", Catherine spoke with a light animated smile. "I have some warm water on the stove and there is a wash basin in the bedroom you may use. I bathed the children in the old cast iron tub and you are welcome to use that as well," she added. Jennie's cheeks flushed pink as she looked into the room with the tub. "I will just freshen up with the wash basin, Catherine, thank you".

As Jennie stood in front of the mirror, staring into her pale blue eyes, she felt like someone had broken into her life and seized the only bit of Lizzy she had left. She knew that Catherine realized that her children wore dead Lizzy's clothes. Now, a stranger had washed Lizzy's clothes and dressed her children. It felt like an intrusion. She didn't want to share that secret part of her life with anyone. Apprehensively, Jennie splashed some warm water on her face. Try as she could, she couldn't wash away that sentiment.

Catherine came to the doorway of the room where Jennie was washing up. She spoke delicately. "Jennie, you probably know what I want to ask you", she said. Jennie raised her face to the mirror and looked into her own eyes again for a response to Catherine's comment. She hesitated, looked into Catherine's face and said, "Yes, I know you must have questions." Catherine took a deep breath and continued "I understand that you want to keep the memory of your first daughter alive. Any mother would want to do the same. But, Jennie, what is this obsession doing to your other children?" Jennie's eyes flashed at Catherine. Her stern face returned, "My children are my business, Catherine. We will be leaving here as soon as we can get the other wagon repaired". Catherine backed away from the doorway with her head lowered. "I thought we could just talk about this quietly while everyone was out of the house, Jennie". "I am sorry to have offended you", Catherine added.

Jennie lowered herself to the chair in the kitchen. Sitting straight backed, she looked at Catherine and said "I have my reasons for what I do, Catherine. My children will understand one day why I do things in my own way. I take good care of them".

CHAPTER 12

CRIPPLED WAGON REPAIR

Perry and Augustine made their way back to the crippled wagon with three horses. Augustine was able to put together enough tools to mend the bent rim of the wheel. It took all the strength of both men to right the wagon wheel. Perry had moved the heavy sacks of flour and feed to the functioning wagon before he left the campsite. He scanned the campsite for any remaining items that may have been missed. Glancing at the flattened grassy spot on the ground where he and Jennie spent the night together, he reminisced being wrapped in each other's arms the night after the storm. If it took the storm to bring them together again, it was worth the trouble, he reflected. Augustine could see that Perry was lost in thought staring at the ground. He rested against the wagon to take a drink of water from his saddlebag and offered a drink to Perry. "C'mon, let's take a break, Perry", he said. Perry tipped his hat back on his head and thanked Augustine for his help. "I didn't know if I would get this old buggy up and going again. My family is thankful to you and Catherine for all you have done for us. Now with Jennie back with us, I figure we should head north to Sheridan".

Augustine stretched his neck back and to the side to limber up. "About those children of yours, Perry, Catherine talked to me about them." Perry interrupted Augustine "I know Jennie has raised the children in an odd way, Augustine. I hope when we get to Sheridan we can get things worked out. She needs to leave our first daughter behind in Cherry Creek and spend some good time with the ones we have with us. I appreciate you wanting to help me out with this but the children are Jennie's worry for now and my goal is to get us on to Sheridan. I don't know what else to say." Augustine patted Perry on the shoulder and said "Its okay friend, I just thought if you wanted to talk, I could be a good listener. Let's get this wagon rigged up with these horses. They've been lazy too long here".

Perry climbed onto the wagon. As the rig lumbered along the dirt trail his mind wandered to Sheridan, Wyoming ahead of him. He would be close to the Big Horn Mountains and there should be good hunting and fishing there and he hoped to find a homestead where his family could do some farming. Even though Cherry Creek was situated at about five thousand feet elevation, the crops were good and there was plenty of water. He hoped Sheridan would have decent enough climate even though it would be another 400 or so miles north of Cherry Creek. He wondered about the winters. Perry was ready to take Jennie and the children north to their new home. He just needed to get there to stake his claim. More than anything though, he wanted to get Jennie to a place where Lizzy didn't linger. He needed to get the children away from Lizzy as well. But, there was still the matter of Lizzy's clothes to reckon with.

CHAPTER 13

CATHERINE'S COUNSEL

The conversation with Catherine ended abruptly. The subject was closed. Catherine respected Jennie's desire not to discuss the children any further. Little Jessica was back to good health now. Watching through the window, Jennie could see her children playing in green grassy yard. She looked at Catherine. "Where did you get the snake bite medicine you gave to Jessica?" Catherine responded in a matter of fact tone. "I got the medicine from an Indian woman" she said. "We were on our way to the Casper mercantile, and a young Indian man approached us on horseback and told us his mother was very ill. Augustine was alarmed when I told the young man to take me to his mother. We found her wrapped in blankets in a campsite not far from here and brought her back here to the house. I did nothing more than give her warm broth and cool compresses until she had enough strength to ride away with her son. We were surprised when the woman returned in spring time and brought several items to us including a snake bite tincture. I have kept it on the shelf in case one of our horses needed it but never dreamed that I would use it on a beautiful child one day". With a faint smile Jennie said, "I met that young Indian man on the prairie. He rode with three other men and caught sight of me hiding in the sagebrush. He didn't indicate to the others that he had seen me. As they were riding away he dropped a pouch of water for me and returned alone the next morning with food. He told me that a white woman had saved his mother from illness and he was returning the favor in honor of his mother. He is the one who led me to your home. I could still be lost out there if it wasn't for him. Your goodness has now saved the Indian woman, saved our Jessica and it has ultimately saved me as well." Catherine sat in silence with her hands folded in her lap as she listened to Jennie's story. Speaking softly, she said "Jennie, I have been blessed many times over in this desolate place and you have been richly blessed as well. Perry and your children are your greatest blessing. The loss of your first child was tragic. She will always be with you till the day you leave this earth. Be strong and true."

Catherine's words to Jennie struck hard. She knew that everything Catherine said was true. Jennie had built a wall around her feelings when Lizzy died. With the birth of each child after Lizzy, she believed the pain of the loss would diminish. Vera, Iris and Jessica were dear to her heart but they did not replace Lizzy, who seemed to always come first in Jennie's days and nights.

CHAPTER 14

THE SECRET LEFT IN MIDDLE BEAR

Augustine arrived back at the house on Middle Bear before Perry. Although the wagon was back on its wheels, the going was slower with the bent wheel rim. Perry had time to think about all that had happened in the past few days and believed that his family would be stronger from the experience. He felt new warmth returning to his Jennie. This trip and the unfortunate events that had ensued had somehow brought them closer than they had been in years. He was ready to continue the trip to Sheridan.

When Perry arrived in Middle Bear, he found Jennie preparing the other wagon for the trip. She was repacking the wagon and organizing their supplies. Jennie seemed subdued in her tasks. Something had happened in his absence to initiate this mood in his Jennie. When he tried to engage Jennie in conversation, she scarcely responded to him. This was the Jennie from Cherry Creek and he was disappointed to see that Jennie return. This was not the time to try and mend any hurt feelings so Perry set about packing the repaired wagon. Augustine and Catherine brought sacks of flour and beans to the Duncan's for their trip. They insisted that the bags be packed in the wagons. Perry argued in vain that they were going to restock in Casper but his complaints went unanswered. They would be ready to head north at daylight tomorrow.

Catherine prepared a festive evening meal with tender beef, potatoes, steamed carrots and freshly made bread. The children devoured their meal with abandon while Catherine smiled across the table watching them. Perry and Augustine discussed the weather and prospective route to Sheridan. Augustine was familiar with the route to avoid deep water crossing of the Platte River near Casper and the Powder River farther north. He told Perry that the Powder River was rarely deep enough to pose any crossing problems unless there was a rain storm over the Big Horn Mountains that increased the water flow on downstream. He prepared a hand drawn map for Perry after dinner. Jennie was silent during the meal, glancing up from her plate occasionally. Catherine light heartedly amused the children with stories about the animals near Middle Bear and encouraged them to watch for coyote, bald eagles and fox along the trail.

Proudly presenting wild plum pie after dinner was eaten; Catherine announced that the present company was the most welcome she had ever had in her home. The cozy home on Middle Bear was filled with warmth of cheerful people that night.

When pie was finished, Catherine rose from the table and began carrying dishes to the kitchen wash basin. Jennie popped out of her chair and gathered her children's dishes. She instructed the children to leave the table and sit in the other room with a large wooden couch and horse hair over- stuffed chairs. One by one the children congregated in the spacious room and sat on the floor beside the fireplace. Jessica's arm, bandaged from the snake bite, was still swollen. Bruising swirled like dark blue ribbons beyond the bandage from the injected venom. Perry and Augustine were immersed in conversation about the trip. Perry's voice was vigorous and full of anticipation for the upcoming trek to northern Wyoming. Jennie watched him from the corner of her eye as she busied herself with clearing the table. She wanted to join the conversation but kept her thoughts to herself for now. She hadn't told Perry about the young Indian man who was responsible for her safe return to Middle Bear. There hadn't come a time when she could talk to Perry alone since her return. Jennie felt like everything that had happened since the snake bite seemed like a dream anyway. She remembered well the bitter night alone on the shadowy prairie. The silence of that night stayed with her thoughts. She felt closer to Lizzy that night under the starry sky and silver gash of a moon. Even though Jennie was getting farther away from Lizzy in the ground, she could not break away from the child left in Cherry Creek. Jennie's thoughts turned morbid as she contemplated that she should have brought Lizzy's pine box casket with her. She knew that Perry would not have allowed that to happen. Perry was careworn to go along with Jennie's insistence on dressing the children in Lizzy's clothes. Jennie wondered if dressing the children in Lizzy's clothes would come to an end once they arrived in Sheridan.

Morning light burst through the east windows of the house on Middle Bear. Catherine and Augustine were outside feeding the animals before the Duncan family stirred from sleep. Jennie, Perry and the children, covered with wool blankets and fleece pelts, were snuggled together in the tiny spare room. It was unusual for Perry and Jennie to sleep past dawn. On this prairie morning the family slept soundly like a litter of sleepy pups. Jennie's eyes fluttered open. In the dimly lit room she slowly rose to one elbow to locate a pathway through the resting bodies. Beside her, Perry had not moved since he lowered himself to the floor in his long threadbare johns. Jennie felt a sense of hopeful expectation. She laid her head back down and listened to the sound of her children and Perry's soft breathing. She could hear Catherine and Augustine's muffled voices outside as they worked together in the corrals. Today she would leave Catherine with long- held secrets. She would mount the wagon with her children and leave Middle Bear.

CHAPTER 15
THE TURNING EVENT

After a hearty breakfast of flapjacks and bacon, the Duncan family readied for their trip. Perry swooped his giggling children, one by one into Jennie's wagon. Grasping Augustine's muscular hand, Perry shook hard. "Thank you, friend", he said. Jennie stood timidly at Catherine's side. She looked into her face and said softly "Catherine, you have done so much for us and I thank you. Jessica may not have survived without your help." Catherine took Jennie's hands into hers and held them tight. "Jennie, your children are very special. I am happy that we had this time with you and with them. Remember what I told you about your children. Jennie smiled and turned to her wagon. Standing next to the wagon, Perry hoisted Jennie up to the wooden seat. Clutching the reins, she looked straight ahead and headed north, leaving Lizzy behind again.

Jennie's wagon rocked rhythmically along the trail. All three of the children dozed perched against the flour sacks piled three high. Jennie could hear Perry whistling behind her as she moved forward. Casper was still three or four days head. If she hurried her horses she might make the trip shorter. She pulled her bonnet rim lower over her eyes as the sun rose higher in the sky and reached down to touch her burlap wrapped gun, secured under the seat.

Late afternoon shadows speckled the prairie. The terrain was hillier the farther north the wagons rolled. The horses showed weariness as they pulled the heavy rigs up the hills near Cottonwood Creek. Perry whistled one loud chirp to alert Jennie to halt her horses. Jumping off his wagon, Perry came to Jennie's wagon and told her that it was about time to pull up for the night. "It looks like there is a protected area over the next hill where we can camp tonight", he said. Jennie nodded. Three little heads peeked around the corner of the canvas topped wagon to see their Pa.

As the wagons topped the next hill, Jennie jerked the reins unexpectedly bringing the wagon to a dead stop. At the bottom of the hill was a covered wagon parked next to a small creek just off the trail. Jennie could see people around the wagon and a campfire burning next to the wagon. Children were chasing and running nearby. Perry arrived quickly at Jennie's wagon as she watched the activity at the bottom of the hill. "Jennie, don't be afraid to continue down the trail. There is safety in numbers here and we can camp beyond the other wagon. We need the water as much as the others and this is a good spot to stop for the night," he said. Jennie flashed a frown to her husband then agreed to move her wagon forward. As the wagons approached the bottom of the hill, two men, two women and three young boys stood watching Jennie and Perry's wagons approach.

Jennie stopped her wagon just past the strangers' wagon while Perry walked over to talk to the men standing near their campfire. After a brief conversation, Perry walked to Jennie's wagon and told her that they would pull their rigs just beyond the parked wagon and set up for the night. Vera, Jessica and Iris shuffled in their places anxious to exit the wagon. "You all stay next to the wagon. Don't be running off getting into trouble", Jennie barked to her children as she stepped down from her seat. Perry arrived at that moment and brought the children to the ground. Captivated by the sight of three ruddy haired, freckled faced boys standing next to Jennie, the Duncan children froze in place. One of the young boys stepped forward and said "We are going fishing for brook trout! Can you come with us?" Jennie stepped between the boys and her children and said "We have to get unloaded and have some dinner. The children can't leave the camp now". The three young boys nodded, turned and ran toward their camp. Their laughter hung in the air as they jumped over boulders and bushes. Perry watched and listened from a distance. His children's eyes tracked the running youngsters back to their campsite. Closing his eyes, he shook his head. He hoped for his children to join the others. He wanted more than anything for his children to run, play and fish. At that moment Perry needed to tell Jennie that she was wrong to keep the children from having fun. He wanted to tell her that it wasn't fair to keep his children sequestered from the world; however, he kept quiet. There was much to be done to unload supplies from the wagon, gather wood for the fire and bring out food and cooking utensils. Jennie tried to keep the children busy running to the wagon and bringing supplies back to her. Her children were distracted by the laughter the youngsters were engaged in at the other campsite. Jennie called to her children to finish their chores. They were lost in the world of the neighboring campsite, not hearing their mother's voice calling to them. Collectively, they were mesmerized by the neighboring youngsters' games and laughter.

Dusk was settling in over the two wagons in the valley. A modest dinner had been prepared and eaten. Jennie prepared the bedrolls for the children. Feeding the horses and tying up a drag line for the night, Perry's mood was somber. "Now can you come and play?" a young voice called from nearby. Jennie's children jumped to their feet from their fireside stools. Perry called out, "They can play till it gets too dark to see ". His children, astonished by their father's loud response, looked to their mother for approval. Jennie glared in Perry's direction but said nothing. Vera and Jessica looked back and forth at their parents. "Follow me!" The young voice shrieked. Grasping their long skirts, Perry's children sailed airborne as they chased off into the early evening.

Jennie said nothing as she finished preparing the children's' beds for the night. When she finished, she sat motionless atop the wagon seat staring into the twilight. Perry walked to the side of the wagon and looked up at her. "Jennie, you can't keep the children away for others forever", he said with a heavy sigh. "I know, Perry", was her response. Jennie's expression was troubled more than angry but she felt both emotions. Perry rarely overturned her instructions to the children and she realized that this may be the beginning of Perry's intention to take control of her attempts to "protect" the children from outside influence. Perry's voice grew stronger. "How can they be out there with other children always mindful they are not the children you want them to be? It is wrong, Jennie. It has to stop." Jennie turned away from Perry's gaze. She knew Perry was right.

Shrieks of delight echoed in the narrow valley as the children scampered near the creek. Jessica and Iris held fishing rods on the bank of the creek while Vera ventured into the water.

Jumping from stone to stone on the creek, Vera slipped and fell into the water soaking every bit of clothing above and below the waist. One of the boys from the other camp ran to help Vera climb out of the water. Vera was lying flat in the creek with legs straight in the air by the time he arrived to help. Staring wide-eyed at Vera's exposed under parts; he reached out his hand, "My name's Joe", the youngster said. Vera stood up wringing creek water from the long skirt. "Why do you wear this skirt?" he murmured pulling his hand from Vera. Dripping wet, Vera said "Ma says I have to". Joe backed away and ran to join the others, glancing curiously back at Vera.

Perry whistled loudly and called for the children to return to the camp. Rosy cheeked and breathless, the children turned up. "Jessica called back to the new friends, "See you tomorrow!" Vera ambled slowly back into camp. Perry looked at Vera and said "Let's get those wet clothes off." Vera whimpered "I didn't mean to fall in the water, Pa. Joe asked me why I wear this skirt, Pa". As Perry helped Vera remove the heavy wet skirt, he asked Vera quietly, "Where are you knickers, Vera?" The child snapped back, "I hate those, Pa. I won't wear those." Saying nothing more, Perry stripped the remainder of wet clothing off Vera and hung them on a cottonwood tree branch. He wrapped Vera in a blanket and carried the child to the wagon.

Perry's heart pounded in torment. What should have been an evening of adventure and fun for Vera turned out to be one of crushing humiliation. Crouched alone by the fire, Perry felt rage gathering in him. His ONLY daughter Lizzy was buried in Cherry Creek River. He felt ashamed to have gone along with the charade as long as he had. He was torn between his love for Jennie and his love for his children. He felt that if Jennie could get away from Cherry Creek she would leave Lizzy at rest in Colorado. The game was over. Jennie's secret was out. Realization hit hard now for Perry. He was a cohort in this lie that Jennie perpetuated. He had been drawn in to the worst situation that a father could have found himself in; yet, he allowed the untruth to continue.

Passion built up in his chest. Perry leapt up from the fireside and dashed to the wagon where his children were tucked into their bed rolls; He flung himself madly onto the wagon, seized their dresses hanging from pegs, and hurled them into the air. Like ruffled parachutes, the dresses floated to the ground. Clutching each other, Perry's youngsters sprung upright, watching in trepidation at behavior they had never seen in their Pa. Perry's rage had been too long entrapped. He could no longer contain this festering anger toward Jennie for what she had brought upon his children.

His frantic face glowed yellow in the firelight as he bound from the wagon running toward Jennie's silhouette beyond the campfire. She stepped backwards as Perry bounded toward her. She too had never seen Perry in such rage. When his feet came to a standstill facing Jennie, he yelled. "Woman, this is over. My SONS will never wear Lizzy's clothes again. Dropping his voice to a coarse whisper, he hissed as he clutched her arm, "Do you understand what I am saying?" Covering her face with trembling hands, she backed further away. Perry turned abruptly and walked back to his wagon. As he passed his sons, he looked into their shadowed frightened faces, pointed to them and said, "You're starting a new life tomorrow, sons. Go to sleep now." Vera, Jessica and Iris looked to their mother's faint outline beyond the fire. They listened to her hushed sobs as they burrowed deep into their bedrolls.

CHAPTER 16

A NEW DAY FOR THE DUNCANS

As daylight crowned over the hill, Perry's sons emerged from their warm cocoons attentive to a commotion in Perry's wagon. Peering around the corner of the wagon top, they saw their Pa amassing a pile of his worn clothing. Sensing that he was being watched, Perry glanced up to see his sons' tiny heads stacked above each other watching him. Gathering the pile of clothing, he carried it to the boy's wagon and said, "You'll be wearing these clothes until we get to the Mercantile in Casper", he said calmly. With a subtle grin, Perry returned to his wagon and came back to his sons with large metal shears. Laying each pair of overalls flat, he chopped the bottoms off. He did the same to his long cotton shirt sleeves. His children stood in wonder at their father's maniacal cutting. After each piece of clothing was cut, he handed the item to each boy and told them to put the clothing on. He handed each of the boys a length of sisal rope to tie the trousers on to their tiny waists. "Where is Ma ?", Vera asked. Perry surveyed the area and said, "Ma will be back soon". The boys tittered as they pulled the worn overalls over their bony white legs. They were lost in the first occasion of wearing man's clothing. After wearing Lizzy's soft ruffled clothing all their lives, they were spellbound, each stroking the coarse fabric of their "new" overalls.

Perched on a stump near the fire, still clutching the heavy metal shears, Perry called his sons to himself. Vera, standing tall in front of his father, beamed with pride in his baggy, frayed dungarees. Perry gently grasped Vera's shoulders and turned the child around, grasped his long curly hair in a single thick bundle and chopped it off just below the ears. He handed Vera the long locks. Vera stared at the hair in his hand and turned to his brothers in disbelief. Iris and Jessica's eyes grew large in astonishment. In unison, the three boys twisted around surveying the campsite to see if their Ma could see what was happening. Distracting them from their search for Jennie, Perry said, "Iris, you are next". Little Iris stepped forward with heightened anticipation and twirled around in front of his father. Next Jessica hurried to his father and did the same. Wondering what to do next, the boys stood together looking to Perry, holding the long curls in their hands. Perry smiled at his boys knowing that the events of this prairie morning were, at best, unsettling. "Do whatever you want with the hair", he murmured. Jessica stuffed his tuft of curls in the large pocket of his overalls which hung low between his knee and ankle. Iris and Vera flung the hair into the air and watched as it separated and floated to the ground.

Gathering the boys in a circle, Perry said in a hushed tone, "Come over and sit with me." Following their father, they sat attentively in a half- circle around Perry. "Today, something else about each of you will be different. This may be hard for you at first, but you will get used to the change. From this day forward, Vera, your name is VERE. Iris, your name is IKE. Jessica, your name is now JESSE." Wide eyed, the Duncan boys gazed up to their father, thunderstruck.

Perry rose to his feet and walked away. The youngsters sat pensively in their crumpled saggy clothing, scrutinizing each other's new identities. Pointing to his brothers, Vere hesitantly announced. "I am Vere. You are Jesse. You are Ike! What will Ma think about our new names?" he questioned. The new Duncan boys sat paralyzed as they contemplated what had happened to them this morning.

"We have to get moving, sons", Perry called out. Jumping up from their places, the boys looked to Perry for guidance. "We need to get this fire stoked for breakfast",

Vere nervously scanned the area in search of his mother. "Pa, where is Ma?" he asked. Perry knelt to the ground, took Vere by the shoulders, looked into his face and said, "Son, your Ma will be back soon. Stop fretting about this." Vere tearfully answered "Ma is going to think we were bad, Pa". Perry stood up, looked down to his son's heartrending expression. "You'll be fine, son. Everyone will be fine." Perry whispered.

Ike and Jesse kicked the dirt and hopped away from camp. They watched for the neighboring camp boys to show up as they did the night before. Vere was restless to show off his boy clothes to the youngster who called himself Joe. "I want Joe to come over again to see us." He told Jesse. Vere wanted to redeem himself to the young boy who helped him rise from the cold creek water the night before. He wanted Joe to see him without long hair but most importantly, he wanted Joe to see him not wearing Lizzy's clothes.

Off in the distance, Jennie appeared on a stony gray ridge. Perry watched her as she slowly approached the campsite. Heaving his shoulders back, he walked in her direction. Each step he took was solid and deliberate. His sons watched their father meet their mother on this early prairie morning like no other morning they knew. Perry stood tall with his hands by his side facing Jennie. His voice rumbled in the stillness of the morning. Jennie, facing Perry, stood frozen. She covered her ears and shook her head at what her husband was saying. Jennie turned and ran to the campsite where her children stood nervously together. When she reached the boys, she gasped. "What has he done to you?" she sneered through her teeth. Backing away from their mother, they seized each other's hands. Watching what was happening, Perry slowly walked to Jennie's side. He took Jennie's arm, turned her away from the boys and looked into her face. "Enough, Jennie. That is enough". Perry returned to the boys and said, "It's time for breakfast, sons. Gather some firewood." Vere, Ike and Jesse scattered. Each of them glanced back at their father, as they set about their tasks. Jennie stormed back to her wagon and warily gathered Lizzy's clothes from the ground where Perry had tossed them. Carefully, she folded the skirts and dresses and held them to her bosom.

CHAPTER 17

JENNIE STAYS BEHIND

Breakfast was eaten in silence. Jennie's boys looked back and forth between their parents and they looked at each other with curious anxiety during their meal. Perry broke the silence with an announcement that the boys would be riding in his wagon for the rest of the trip. "We'll be putting most of the supplies in Ma's wagon", he said loudly. Biting her lip, Jennie looked at Perry with contempt. Perry didn't give Jennie a chance to speak. "Let's get this camp cleaned up and be ready to leave", he said cheerfully. Jumping up from the campfire, the young boys ran to their father's wagon.

Jennie remained seated at the campfire while her boys and Perry busied themselves gathering supplies to put into Jennie's wagon. She stared at the tin plates from breakfast scattered on the ground around the fire. Rising from the rotted stump seat, she sauntered away leaving the dishes planted in their places. Perry watched his wife as she wandered off toward the creek. For a moment he had a notion to follow her, but shook off the desire to try and console her. The events of the past hours gave him rationale to stand his ground and focus on his sons. Jennie would have to accept the changes that had taken place. At this point, neither he nor the boys approached Jennie.

When Jennie's wagon was packed with most of the supplies that had been removed from Perry's wagon, Perry instructed the boys to gather the breakfast dishes and take them to the creek to wash. Each child gathered his own plate. Vere took Perry and Jennie's plate in his hand, looked up at this father and said, "Ma is at the creek now, Pa. Should we wait till she is not there anymore?" Perry understood that his sons were apprehensive about facing their mother. "We can put these dishes in a sack and wash them when we get to our next camp", Perry chirped. His boys looked at each other in amazement. Life felt different for them on this morning.

"Let's get loaded up, sons" Perry called out. One by one the boys boosted themselves on to their father's wagon. Once seated, they wiggled on their seats in nervous excitement. Perry went to the creek to fill the water jugs. He advanced toward Jennie as she sat by the water and told her they were ready to head north. Jennie did not respond to Perry's announcement. "We'll be starting out now, Jennie, "he called out to her. "Your wagon is packed and ready." When Jennie refused to acknowledge his presence, Perry turned and walked up the hill lugging the heavy water jugs. Instead of storing both full water jugs in Jennie's wagon with the other supplies, he placed one of them in the wagon with his sons. He also loaded one of his two rifles into his wagon and left one in Jennie's. Sitting tall on the worn wooden seat, Perry pulled his hat low over his forehead, cracked the whip and jerked the wagon forward. In hushed surprise, Perry's sons turned to see their mother perched creek side alone. Perry tilted his head back to his boys and yelled "Ma will be coming along when she is ready. Keep a lookout for coyotes and rabbits ".

Periodically, each of the boys leaned over the side of the wagon and looked back to see if their mother was behind them. Vere crawled up to sit next to his father and said "Ma isn't behind us yet, Pa. Should we wait for her?' Perry casually answered "Ma is taking her time, son. She'll come along when she is ready." Peering around the side of the wagon for another quick look back, he jumped back to be with his brothers. As time went by the boys spent less time searching the trail behind for their mother. Perry didn't look back even once.

Back at the creek, Jennie stirred from her place by the gurgling water. She heard Perry's wagon leave but had not moved from her place. Dipping her hands in the ice cold water, she splashed her face. Alone again, she sat motionless. The difference was that she knew that Perry was not looking for her this time. She knew that she had isolated herself from her family both physically and emotionally. The sound of the horses' restless snorting at her wagon brought her to her senses.

CHAPTER 18
A SILENT TRIP

Jennie climbed to the top of the ridge above her resting place by the creek. She grasped at ragged rocks and dried sagebrush branches to balance her. When her tired legs carried her to the top of the ridge, she glanced around. The neighboring wagon was still tucked into the cottonwoods draw. She listened to the voices coming from their campsite. Hoisting herself on to her packed wagon, she felt her heart heavy and slow to beat. Pressing the horses forward, she delivered a slow motion jerk of the reins. Glimpsing the two track dirt trail snaking through the hills ahead, Jennie noted that Perry's wagon was out of sight now. Reaching under the splintered seat, she grasped her burlap wrapped gun and buried it deep in her skirt pocket. For just one day, Jennie wanted to forget what she was leaving behind and think about what good things could be ahead for her. She remembered how Catherine had reminded her of how lucky she was to have such wonderful children and a good husband. Recalling Perry's rage toward her now, she felt miserable for the bitter exchange between them.

CHAPTER 19

A FATHER'S FIRST NOTION

Perry's wagon lumbered along the trail toward Casper Mountain. No other wagons had passed him heading south. He caught sight of the Platte River bending around a far off ridge and calculated that he might stop there to give his sons lunch. When the trail took a hard right turn around a rock outcropping, Perry finally glanced back to see if Jennie's wagon was in sight. It crossed his mind that she may have headed back to Cherry Creek.

Feeling as if a heavy stone was lodged in his gut, he sought mental justification for leaving Jennie behind. How could he have allowed Jennie to perpetrate this unimaginable life for his young sons for so long? It haunted him to reflect that the boys had been wearing Lizzy's clothes from birth. When each of the three sons was born, Jennie's eyes filled with disappointment at the news that she had given birth to another son. Jennie isolated the boys from neighbors in Cherry Creek. The boys still talked in an odd sort of "baby talk" as they grew. They only conversed with each other. Jennie was sparse with her conversation with her sons and forbid them to talk to anyone unless she was present. She was schooling them at home as time permitted. They were bright and obedient but were growing up in seclusion from the outside world. Jennie's bizarre mental circumstance had created a life of deception and confusion for her husband and children that seemed unescapable. Perry considered that if he hadn't intervened now, the chaos would only amplify. With resolve, he pressed his wagon ahead. Surely a new life awaited them in Sheridan, with, or without Jennie. He was not about to return to the life of bizarre deception that he and his young sons were caught up in on the homestead in Cherry Creek.

The Platte River curved and twisted through the rolling hills north of Wheatland. Perry saw several places along the river where it looked like wagons had crossed the river in the past. He remembered what Augustine had told him about finding a shallow crossing area. The Platte was mostly a calm river but had some deep areas that would envelop a wagon within a few feet of the bank. Following the most traveled trail to the river's edge, he pulled the wagon to a flat grassy area for lunch. Anxious to get off the wagon, the Duncan boys headed for the river. Perry cautioned them to stay at the bank of the river until he could be with them. "Maybe after lunch we could take a swim in the river", he called to the boys as they ran down the slope to the river's edge. When the boys reached the bank of the river, Perry listened to their squeals of delight echoing off the water. He looked back along the trail searching for any sign that Jennie might be coming behind. No sign of Jennie's wagon was visible.

The hot Wyoming summer sun, high overhead, beat hard on Perry's boys' heads today. Their tender scalps were no longer covered by long hair and Lizzy's large brimmed bonnets. Walking slowly to the bank of the Platte River, he watched his "newborn" sons in wonder. He had never given much thought to teaching them to fish and hunt. He too was caught up in the pretention of Jennie's upbringing of the boys. Unaccustomed to seeing the children in clothes other than Lizzy's dresses; he found it bewildering how he had gradually accepted the madness of it all. His father once told him that a frog could be placed in a pot of water and as the heat was slowly turned up the frog would not realize the water was at the boiling point, would not attempt to jump out and would perish in the pot. He was like the frog in the water as far as his sons' future was concerned. The water had reached the boiling point. The boy at the campsite who discovered that "Vera" was actually a boy under the long skirt was essentially the tipping point for both Vere and Perry. Perry was sad to recall his young son's humiliation when his identity was questioned by the boy at the creek. He vowed that this would never happen again to his sons. When he left Cherry Creek, he had three daughters as far as the neighbors knew. Now he would live in Wyoming with three sons. A new life awaited the Duncan boys in Wyoming. Perry smiled as he watched his raggedly dressed sons pitching stones across the river. He noticed a curious change in his sons' demeanor. It was remarkable to watch them interact so differently. Freed from the constraints of the cumbersome clothing, the Duncan boys' lives took on new explorations. Perry craved this wondrous moment to last. Jennie could not take this bliss away from him or his sons. It was theirs from this time on.

CHAPTER 20

RIFLE THEFT

Perry's harsh words reverberated over Jennie's mind as her wagon moved along the trail toward the Platte River. She was at least two hours behind Perry and the children but didn't push the horses to a faster pace. She wondered how she would react when meeting up with her family. Was it a feeling of remorse that engulfed her? It felt more like anger but she wasn't sure if the anger was toward Perry or toward herself. In one moment she felt incensed at Perry's behavior and in the next moment she was filled with powerful fear. Jennie halted her wagon and examined the dreary surroundings. Is this the time to circle the wagon back to Cherry Creek? All that was left there was Lizzy in the pine box.

Tossing her dusty bonnet to the wagon floor, Jennie gathered her hair and wrapped and twisted it on top of her head. Sweat had dampened the back of her neck and her forehead in the afternoon heat. Turning back to Cherry Creek now seemed a preposterous solution. She was strong and capable. Folks in Cherry Creek often remarked at Jennie's strength and determination in raising her three "girls" after Lizzy died. Jennie showed the world that she would survive the loss and be a good mother to her children in spite of her grief. With staunch resolve, she pushed the horses ahead toward the Platte River.

As time passed, Jennie let the horses lead the wagon on the trail. The reins rested lightly in her hands as she dozed in the warm sun. Violently from behind, in a furious upheaval, four galloping horses with riders hurtled to the side of the wagon in a wild explosion of dust. Jennie's horses startled, throwing their heads back.

The reins jerked from Jennie's hands. She frantically reached to retrieve them from the floor board. Instantly she recognized one of the riders as the young Indian man whom she had met on the prairie. The red feathers in the horse mane fluttered as he jerked his horse to a halt. Her heart pounded in the veins in her neck as she struggled to regain control of her horses. When she got the wagon stopped, she looked into the face of the young Indian man and saw him delicately shake his head as if to quiet any recognition. Slipping her hand into the secret skirt pocket, she touched the gun while she sat waiting for some indication of the intentions of the men. Among the intruders there was discussion which Jennie did not understand. The young man remained silent but watched Jennie intently. "What do you want?" Jennie blurted in a loud deep voice that even she didn't recognize. The young man moved his horse closer to the wagon. It became evident to Jennie that he would interpret his legions' message. Jennie looked into the eyes of the young man who had rescued her from the prairie heat. He diverted his eyes away to keep from making any further eye contact with her. "We want guns you have in your wagon", he said coldly. Jennie jumped off the wagon to the ground and motioned for the young man to board her wagon. "Take what you want from my wagon ", she said weakly. One of the older Indian men dismounted from his horse and walked in Jennie's direction. Stepping in front of Jennie, the young Indian held his hand out to separate Jennie from the older man. At that point Jennie dropped to the ground, clutched her stomach and vomited. The young man spoke angrily to the others in his native language. Jennie looked up as the older man backed away from her. Bathed in streaks of dusty sweat and vomit, her pale face furrowed in sobs. The young Indian man boarded Jennie's wagon, shuffled around inside and emerged carrying the long rifle which Perry had intentionally left for Jennie.

He held the gun high over his head for the others to see. No further words were spoken. Turning their horses, the riders left Jennie. The young Indian man, once again, glanced back at Jennie still crumpled on the ground. As she rose from the dirt, Jennie's trembling hand reached for the gun deep in her pocket. She began to lift her weapon from its hiding place but cautiously let it slip back into its hidden location.

Her legs shook violently as she lifted her foot to step to the floor board of the wagon. Her arms grew limp as she grasped the reins. All she wanted in this moment was to be with her family far ahead of her. Hot tears seared down her reddened cheeks. The hazy path that stretched ahead seemed insurmountable to her. Stepping to the back of the wagon, she took some water to her parched throat. Before pushing the horses forward, she threw her shoulders back, brushed the hair from her face and wiped away the salty droplets. Weakness would not serve Jennie well now. She knew she had to gather her wits about her to make her way to her family. If she stayed the course and pushed her team she could catch up with Perry and the children, even if she had to travel into the darkness. Jennie decided she would do whatever it took to find her family.

CHAPTER 21

SHOT IN THE DARK

Long shadows sprouted alongside the trail. Darkness was coming upon Jennie. Her eyes could no longer distinguish which direction the trail faced ahead. The horses hesitated to move at the accelerated pace Jennie was demanding. It seemed to her that hours dragged by as she searched the distance for a glimpse of a campfire. As time went by, Jennie's eyes were darting back and forth across the trail with such rapidity that she felt a light-headed sensation overtaking her.

A minuscule speck of light ahead caught Jennie's eye. It shimmered. It disappeared and reappeared. She couldn't tell how far away it was. Sucking in a short breath, she hastened the horses in spite of the darkness. "Go!" she shouted into the blackness that surrounded her wagon. All she could see was the tiny amber light flickering ahead. Nothing else mattered at that point. She could not lose sight of the light. In small increments, the light grew in size. As the trail turned away from the light, panic set into Jennie's heart. Surely the trail would turn back to face the light again. She pushed the horses faster. As the trail twisted, Jennie turned her head to keep sight of the light. She let the horses lead the way as she kept the light in her line of sight. The lead horse stumbled and slowed in spite of Jennie's insistence. She came to realize that neither she nor the horses had eaten anything since she left the site of the Indian incident. She had pushed her team beyond their endurance.

Pulling on the reins, Jennie stopped the wagon. Fumbling in the darkness, she clumsily felt her way through to the back of the wagon and found a bucket of oats. The bucket handle clanked in her hand as she felt her way to the front of the wagon. Recognizing the sound of the feed bucket, the horses shifted and snorted in the darkness. As she dipped her hand into the bucket, Jennie could sense that the bucket was only half full. The horses were hungry. As she patted her way to the front seat of the wagon, she slid her hands along the side of the wagon to find her way to sideboard step. She jumped to the ground in total blindness. Jennie left the bucket on the side of the seat until her feet touched the ground, then turned and grasped the bucket handle. As she moved alongside the horses, she could feel their warm labored breath in the air beside her. In the darkness she reached into the bucket and held out her hand touching the soft noses of her horses to give them much needed handful of food. She knew that they needed water as well but felt the food would carry them for a short time. The horses stretched their necks to nudge her for more food. She had emptied the bucket after just a few handfuls for each horse.

Sagebrush rustled somewhere near Jennie. Then it rustled louder, closer than before. Chills rippled on the back of her neck. The horses alarmed at the sudden noise in the dark. Jennie couldn't see what whipped in the sagebrush close to her. She thrust her hand into her skirt pocket, grasped her gun and brought it to her chest. Holding her breath, she stood motionless waiting for the next sound. In the ensuing moment, a crushing, weighty blow thumped upon her back and knocked her forward to the ground. As she fell to the ground, a loud gunshot pierced the blackness that surrounded her. It thundered in her ears. The wind was pushed from her lungs as she fell to the ground. A heavy thud shook the ground near her. Stumbling to her feet, she hurdled forward wrapping her arms around the neck of one of the horses. Blinking her eyes wildly, she searched the darkness to perceive what had plummeted to the ground. Did she shoot one of her own horses? The horses shuffled and stomped anxiously as she felt her way to each horse. They were both standing. Suddenly there was movement on the ground. Jennie didn't know which way to move to get away from whatever stirred in the darkness. With her gun still in her hand, she fingered her way around the horses and moved to the front of the team, putting her animals between her and the unknown menace. She could hear a rasping sound on the ground on the far side of her horses. She breathed hard as if she had been running. Her temples pulsed in fear.

A grating sound on the dirt caught Jenney's senses. Was it a claw or was it a hand? Everything had happened so quickly, she struggled to remember what it felt like when she was hit on the back. Could it have been an animal or was it a human who knocked her to the ground? All she discerned was that it was a heavy, powerful blow.

Now there was dark silence. The horses ceased movement. Jennie stood at attention prepared for whatever may come next. She held her gun in front of her with both hands.

She couldn't gauge how much time has passed since she last heard the scraping sound on the dirt. Silence encased her. Her hands shook as her muscles fatigued from holding the heavy gun in one position. Her imagination began to swirl in dizzying confusion. What was lying on the ground next to the wagon? Who or what did she shoot? Why did this person or creature attack her from behind? How could she have left her seat on the wagon without lighting a lantern to feed the horses? She was in too much of a hurry to follow the tiny light in the distance. There was no light to be seen now. Jennie's legs began to quiver as well as her arms. She slid down the side of one of the horses to rest seated on the ground.

Exhaustion overtook Jennie at some point during the night. She woke with a start as one of the horses shook the morning dew from its back. Dawn had broken over the horizon. Jennie crawled to look through the legs of the horses to the other side of the wagon. Through the dim light Jennie saw nothing on the ground. She rose to her feet, with gun in her hands and slowly walked around the horses. With her gun held out in front of her, she turned from side to side in search of whatever struck her in the night. She found a spot of blood that had mixed with the grey sandy dirt. Whatever had lain in the dirt had been dragged across the trail leaving splatters of blood. Jennie followed the drag marks in the dirt as far as she could see. The marks disappeared with no further indication of where they led. It was as if they had ascended into thin air leaving no further trail.

CHAPTER 22

ESCAPE AT DAWN

As the morning light enhanced, Jennie climbed into her wagon and drug out a full corked jug of water. She gave each of the horses a cupped handful of water then splashed some water on her face. Pacing out from the wagon once again in every direction, she searched for a clue as to what or who came upon her the night before. No clue was left. No footprint, no animal print, just scraped dirt and blood splatter to confirm that Jennie had not dreamt the happenings. The mystery haunted her. It would not leave her mind. Since the entire event happened in pitch blackness, Jennie had no visual point of reference. She could see nothing and her only sense of the event was what she heard and felt. Fearing retribution for what she had done, even though it was done unintentionally, Jennie rationalized her actions. The shot could just as well have struck her or one of her horses.

It was time to leave this place. Heaving the heavy water jug back into the wagon, Jennie seated herself squarely on the wagon seat. Before whipping the horses forward, she investigated her surroundings one last time for clues. Since Jennie arrived at this place in the dark, she had no way to determine if anything looked out of place. Glancing back, she hoped to see some clue as to what happened. Whipping the horses, she left the nightmare behind.

CHAPTER 23

REUNION ON THE PLATTE

Perry Duncan stood on a limestone rise overlooking the Platte River. His weathered hand shaded his eyes from the early morning sun glare. He searched the prairie expanse for any sign of movement in the distance. Restless through the night, Perry rose early while his sons slept soundly in the wagon. He recognized that Jennie needed time to adjust to the enormous shock of shifting her children from daughters to sons. He believed that she would follow close behind him on the trail. Stoking the campfire with dew dampened sage branches was his way of signaling to Jennie their location. He lingered on the rise looking for some sign that she was close behind.

The Duncan boys stirred in the wagon. Ike was the first child to emerge with his treasured man clothes bunched up in his arms. He hurriedly jumped from the wagon and dressed in the chilly morning air. Perry noticed the look of satisfaction on Ike's face as he tucked his ragged shirt tail into his saggy pants. Perry smiled as Ike ran to his side, his sleepy little face beaming. "When is Ma going to be here, Pa"? Perry said quietly, "Anytime now, son. We'll wait a bit longer. How about you help me to start breakfast?" Ike's eyes lit as he looked up to Perry's face.

Vere and Jesse poured from the wagon with their own gathering of bulky clothing. Humored by his sons' clumsy efforts to dress in the oversized garments, Perry Duncan turned his head to conceal his grin.

Smoke curled above the campsite. Perry instructed the boys to gather sagebrush leaves to throw on the fire. The youngsters couldn't know that the fleshy silver sagebrush leaves would create a more visible white smoke in the air for Jennie to see from a distance. The smoke hung heavily and drifted across the prairie landscape like translucent pale ribbons in the morning sun. As the breakfast preparations continued, Perry glanced out from camp toward the trail. No sign of Jennie's wagon came visible.

With breakfast finished, the youngsters expected that their father would once again encourage them to get packed up for the next part of the journey. Perry handed each of the boys a heavy boar bristle brush and told them to brush down the horses before they left camp. "You need to brush the dust from the horses before we head out", he said. Jesse looked at Perry in surprise saying "But Pa, we usually brush the horses in the evening". Perry motioned Ike to the horses and walked toward the river.

Standing on the bank of the Platte River, Perry looked back at his sons busily brushing the horses. Barely reaching the tops of the legs of the animals, Ike had brought a wooden stump to stand on to reach the flanks of the horses.

Strolling to a section of the river where willows were growing along the bank, Perry sat down, pulled the boots from his feet, stripped his clothes off and walked into the cold running water. Sinking under, Perry laid flat on his back looking into the blue morning sky. He swirled through the water and surfaced face first shaking the frigid water from his hair. As he emerged shivering from the river, he saw his sons standing side by side, brushes in hand, watching their father as he stood naked by the flowing river in the background. Perry flashed a smile their way. These children had never seen their father naked. Wearing Lizzy's clothes somehow kept Perry from seeing his children as the sons they were. They were Jennie's "girls". Perry motioned to the boys to come to the river. The youngsters looked at each other, dropped their brushes to the ground, and ran to the bank of the Platte River by their father. "Time for a bath, sons", Perry called out to them. Reluctantly, they stripped naked and stood waiting for instructions. Standing knee deep in the water, he turned and jumped into the river splashing water onto his sons still standing on the bank. Shrieks of wonder echoed on the river bank that morning as Perry's sons joined him in the rushing water, splashing and jumping on their father's back, Perry's boys were delirious with newfound naked freedom for the first time in their young lives. The Duncan boys' blue lips and fingers from the cold water signaled to Perry that it was time to leave the water. Shivering, the children tiptoed onto the rocky bank and pulled their scruffy clothes on over their icy bodies. Perry had never seen his children so full of bliss. His heart lightened at the sight of their rosy cheeks and shameless smiles.

Chattering like young magpies, they climbed the bank to return to camp. Jesse was the first to reach the summit of the hill and stood motionless gazing into camp. As Perry reached the summit he saw Jennie's wagon parked down the trail not far from camp. Jennie stood waiting for a response from her family. Jesse looked to his father for approval then ran to his mother clutching her leg. Jennie dropped to her knees, burying her face into Jesse's soggy head of hair. Vere and Ike joined their brother. She gathered her children in a bunch on the ground, sobbing and laughing simultaneously. Perry calmly walked toward his family. Jennie rose to her feet. With the young ones still clutching her skirt, she looked into

Perry's face, held out her arms and gathered him in. Perry shook his head and wrapped his arms around his weary Jennie.

His eyes misted gray as he stood holding Jennie. He had long decided he was not leaving camp that day until he had this moment with her in his arms. Unbeknownst to his sons, his procrastination this morning was intentional.

Jennie, quiet and unresponsive, watched her family interact with each other. Her energy was spent during the night. Joining in on family discussions was too tedious for her this day. She didn't have the will to talk about what had transpired over the last hours. All she wanted was to finish the trip to Sheridan with her family. The dark memory of what happened in the night smothered her thoughts. They hindered her steps. Perry noticed her lethargy and tried to uplift Jennie. "We missed you, Jennie. We need you to be with us." Jennie nodded and looked away. How could she explain what happened when she saw nothing? It was too complicated to talk about.

CHAPTER 24

LEAVING THE PLATTE RIVER

The family prepared the wagons for the day's trip north. Perry had been consolidating supplies into Jennie's wagon when he stepped down from the wagon, pulled Jennie aside, and asked her "Jennie, where is the rifle?" "They took it, Perry. Indians came to the wagon and took it". "My God, Jennie, when did this happen? Were you hurt?" Jennie stared ahead, with no emotion in her voice, said calmly; "Nobody was hurt. I just gave it to them when they asked". Perry stood vacuously astonished looking at Jennie. He took her arm in his hand and turned her toward him. "Jennie, you could have been killed". "But I wasn't," she said unmoved. Perry took her by her shoulders and looked her square in the face. "Jennie, do you still have the pistol?" "I have it Perry. I still have it". Perry questioned her again; "Jennie how did you manage to keep the pistol?" Annoyed, Jennie blurted "I had it in my skirt pocket, Perry!" Perry dropped his hands from Jennie's shoulders. He stepped back and closed his eyes. Lunging forward, he enfolded Jennie in his arms, squeezing her so forcefully that she gasped for breath. Burying his face in the nape of her neck, he whispered "Jennie, please, let's get to Sheridan now. Your sons need you, I need you. We have to make this fresh start as a family."

Jennie threw her arms around Perry's neck and held him silently. Perry continued, "Let's put all this behind us, Jennie. Today we start all over. Can you do that?" Jennie hesitated, and then nodded. Lingering in the embrace, Jennie finally pulled away. There was more to tell Perry but she couldn't speak of it just yet. Maybe she would never speak of it again. Maybe it never happened, she thought.

The wagons were precisely packed. Perry organized his wagon to make room for his sons and transferred a few extra supplies into Jennie's wagon. The flour sacks were stacked neatly in a pile next to the dried meat and carefully packed jars of fruit that Jennie canned before leaving Cherry Creek. Jennie noticed that Perry had packed her wagon with all the supplies toward the back and arranged the bedding in a tidy soft pile toward the front of the wagon. The heavy blankets were laid on the floor making a fluffy bed of warmth and feather down. Jennie thought about the night to come. She would sleep beside Perry tonight somewhere on the Wyoming prairie. She flushed at an unfamiliar stirring in her loins.

Turning her wagon toward the trail, Jennie glanced back at Perry's wagon behind her. Perry and Ike sat straight backed on the front seat while Vere and Jesse poked their heads between them. Perry had made a make shift hat from some leather scabbards to protect the tender head of young Vere. The youngster sat tall and proud, a comical sight to Jennie as she took a second look at the child.

As the wagons proceeded toward Casper, Jennie heard snippets of whistling and loud conversation Perry was having with his sons. From time to time, the breeze shifted enough to transmit the voices clearly to Jennie. She was comforted by the presence of Perry's wagon behind her. The sun was warm on her face that morning.

Her cloth bonnet ruffled in the breeze as she moved along the trail. Hours passed in silence while she pushed back thoughts of the gunshot in the darkness. The thoughts returned over and over in spite of her determination to abandon them. Precipitously she came to realize that her compulsive thoughts of Lizzy had been crowded out by the remembrance of the shooting in the night. Jennie knew she had to banish these thoughts from her mind but she did not want to replace them with her familiar grief thoughts of Lizzy back in Cherry Creek again.

A shrill whistle pierced the warm dry air. Jennie halted her wagon and peered back to see Perry dismounting from his perch. Walking to the side of her wagon, he reached up to help her down. Grasping her waist, he carefully transported her to the ground. "We need a break, Jennie", he whispered to her. You need some rest. As he turned away, he brushed her cheek lightly with his fingers. She touched her cheek where Perry's touch felt so warm and sensuous. Removing her bonnet, she hastily stroked her hair to attempt some order to her tousled strands.

One after the other, the young Duncan boys leapt from wagon like baby birds leaving the nest for the first time. Jennie watched in wonder at their lighthearted demeanor. Something much more significant than their clothing had changed for these youngsters. They were her sons now. Jennie believed at that moment that Lizzy's clothes would never be worn again by these children.

The boys were off and running across the prairie, jumping over scattered clumps of lava rock covered with orange and yellow lichens. Watching her young ones, Jennie called out a warning of snakes hiding amidst the rocks and sagebrush. Perry snickered, "No snake will hang around with the ruckus these boys are making, Jennie". Inspecting the foot of one of Jennie's horses, Perry grimaced. "We may have to give this one some rest, Jennie. He is limping some. Maybe we are pushing too hard." Jennie silently remembered how she gave her horses no rest when she was alone with the wagon. She felt a pang of guilt surge across her body as she bent down to stroke her horse's swollen leg. Staring at the leg, her mind wandered to the moment her gun went off. She could never tell Perry about that night. Her anger and resentment had caused so much misery and harm to her husband and children, and now, to one of her dependable horses. If she had gone ahead with Perry and the children instead of languishing behind, none of those grim events would have transpired.

Reaching down, Perry gently lifted Jennie from her crouched position. "Jennie, you have been so quiet since you arrived at camp with us. We will take time to rest the horse. It will be good for all of us to have some time off the trail. When we get to Casper, we will take a day or so to get supplies and get ready for the last leg of the trip. Sheridan is within our reach now, Jennie". He seized Jennie's face in his hands and delicately kissed her forehead. Jennie closed her eyes, smiled and nodded. Her shadowy secret had wrapped around her mind so tightly she could hardly think about Casper or Sheridan. Concealment of the shooting incident was consuming her, yet, she couldn't bring herself to speak of it. It was a preposterous story that even she couldn't quite believe, so how could she expect Perry to do so. It was possible that she had shot a cougar or coyote in the dark. She would leave it at that.

After Perry had applied liniment and wrapped Jennie's horse's leg, he whistled to his sons who came scattered from every direction. Their oversized, sagging pockets bulged heavy with rocks and relics from the prairie floor. Beaming, Jesse opened his hand to show Perry an arrowhead he scavenged from a fire ring on ridge beyond the trail. After showing the arrowhead to his father, he ran to Jennie to show her his treasure. Jennie examined it carefully, overturned it, and rubbed it between her fingers. "Do you like it Ma? You can keep it Ma", Jesse bellowed. Jennie examined the arrowhead, opened Jesse's hand, placed the arrowhead in it, then gently closed his hand and told him to keep it in a safe place for her. Jesse turned and ran back to his father's wagon.

When the boys had loaded into their father's wagon, Perry strolled to Jennie as she waited by her wagon and playfully boosted her to her seat. Holding on to her hand tightly as she was seated, he said, "Our next stop will be for the night, Jennie". He tipped the brim of his hat and winked back at his wife as he turned away. A torrent of heat boiled up to her shoulders and neck as she watched him pace back to his wagon. Perry had a certain look about him today that reminded her of their early times together. She brushed the dust from her skirt, gathered her long hair in a twist on her neck and shook the reins.

CHAPTER 25
VISIT FROM THE SHERIFF

In seemingly slow motion, Jennie's wagon creaked forward. She could feel the reins relaxing lightly in her hands but her mind and body felt transformed today. She wasn't the woman who lived through a night of dreadfulness; the woman who may have slaughtered another person in the black gloom of the lonely prairie. Perusing back to her husband's wagon, she struggled to transport herself back to the perfect sunlit day. Jennie was set upon leaving the past behind her, just as Perry instructed her to do.

Her daydream shadowed her as she traveled the trail. Embracing thoughts of the evening ahead, she longed for Perry to hold her closely. The warm sunshine lulled her mind, warmed her face and soothed her aching muscles.

Perry's loud chirp from behind jolted her to wakefulness. She halted her wagon and abruptly twisted around on her seat. Perry's face was strained. He pointed to the northeast. Jumping from his seat, he sprinted to Jennie's wagon. Before Jennie could look to where Perry was pointing, Perry arms were in the air reaching for Jennie to dismount from her wagon. "Jennie, come back to my wagon and wait with the children", he said. Jennie turned to see a group of horses coming toward them at full gallop. "Jennie, do you have your gun?" Jennie patted her skirt pocket and nodded. "Get in the wagon now, Jennie". Perry nervously looked around his wagon as Jennie jumped aboard. She squeezed into the back of the wagon and placed herself between the children and the entrance. Ike whispered "Mama, what is happening?" Jennie placed her finger over her lips to hush the youngsters and pulled the canvas curtain closed, darkening the inside of the wagon.

Sucking in her breath, Jennie heard commotion outside the wagon. Perry's voice boomed "What can I help you with, men?" A stranger's voice called back "Where are you headed, Mr.? "We're heading north to Sheridan", Perry shouted. Jennie pulled the curtain aside just enough to see three men and Perry standing in a circle near the stranger's horses. Their voices faded into more hushed tones and Jennie couldn't comprehend their conversation. Leaning back against the sideboard, she felt relieved to discern there wasn't any confrontational tone to the discussion. After several minutes Jennie heard Perry's voice more clearly as he moved closer to the wagon. He called out "So Long" to the men.

"Jennie, come on out", Perry muttered outside. Jennie poked her head through the side of the curtain and looked around to see if anyone was with Perry. She cautiously moved to the seat and sat waiting to hear more from her husband. "Those men said there was a shooting somewhere south of here. It seems that a Crow Indian was shot." That was the Sheriff from Cheyenne. He said the tribe was on the hunt for the shooter and we should be watchful". Jennie's face paled as she stared at the ground next to Perry. "Jennie, don't worry, we'll be fine. We'll stay on the trail and we'll stay alert", he whispered. Perry added, "I didn't mention that you had a gun taken from your wagon, Jennie. It didn't seem that I should cause any further discussion about that. For all we know, it could have been the rifle that was taken from you that was used in the shooting and we just don't need to be involved any further. The rifle didn't have any identification marks on it, so we will just let it be. Do you understand, Jennie?" Jennie nodded, looking into Perry's eyes. She sensed that Perry had some suspicion about the whole turn of events. Perry jumped onto the seat next to Jennie, put his arm around her shoulder and wrapped himself around her wilting body. "Let's get back on the trail now and finish this leg of the trip. We'll pull over for the night in a couple hours. We won't wait until dark to settle in".

Jumping off Jennie's wagon, Perry scanned the horizon and lumbered back to his rig. Watching him intently, Jennie's shoulders winced when he glanced back at her. Something in his expression troubled her.

Perry's whistle signaled to move ahead. Jennie led the way with her wagon and team.

The sky had darkened with patchy gray clouds during the brief stop on the trail. Jennie missed the warmth of the sun on her face. Now she felt a cool breeze blowing from the north. She tried to return to the easy-going state of mind she was in before the interruption but couldn't get back to the feeling that everything would work out. There was worry nudging her thoughts now. It *was* a man that had been shot. It wasn't an animal after all. Perry didn't say if the man had been fatally shot. Just shot. Jennie didn't want to know the rest of the story. Over and over, she told herself that she didn't shoot someone on purpose. It wasn't something she set out to do. It just happened. It was an accident. But she also knew that the "accident" may have saved her life. But then again, maybe it was an animal that confronted her in the dark.

The afternoon sun had beaten hard. Now, gray clouds covered to cool the air. Shadows grew longer on the horizon like dark beasts skulking from behind hillsides and crags. Jennie felt fearful of the approaching darkness. Listening for Perry's wagon, she turned to see that it was still behind her. Waiting for Perry to choose a location to spend the night seemed interminable. Her arms hung weary, her heart lay heavy and her mind wandered in fatigue.

As the sun sank closer to the horizon, tiny specks of pink speckled the darkening skies. The air, noticeably cooler, had stilled. Just ahead, Jennie could see a stand of trees in a shallow draw. Jennie would sleep among those trees with Perry this night.

She rushed her wagon to the shady location where she hoped to spend the night. Perry followed behind with three little heads bobbing as the wagon maneuvered over the rutted terrain. The draw was narrow and long with sparsely placed cottonwood and narrow leaf willow trees sprouting from the sides of the draw. Perry dismounted his wagon first and discovered other wagons had spent the night in the same place. A fire ring with rocks and tree stumps were situated in the lower area of the draw shaded by low hanging branches. A frayed strand of sisal twine hung from one of the cottonwood branches.

The Duncan boys wasted no time in leaving the wagon to explore their overnight location. Vere and Jesse led the way following the draw to the west. Perry called out to them telling them to bring back branches for firewood. Standing at the side of Jennie's wagon, Jesse stood waiting for his mother to come down. Jennie climbed off her wagon, knelt down to look her Jesse in the eyes. He wrapped his arms around his mother's neck tightly. "What's bothering you?" she whispered to him. "Ma, stay with us please", he whimpered. Jennie's eyes watered as she looked into her son's face. "I'm not leaving again" she said. "Now go to be with the others". Jesse tugged the waist of his baggy pants, hiked them up and darted off. Watching from a distance, Perry Duncan stood quietly. After Jesse had vanished to join his brothers, Perry approached Jennie. He took her hands in his and pulled her close, resting his lips on Jennie's cheek. Burying his face into Jennie's warm neck, he pulled her body closer. "Jennie, tonight I want to be with you. Tonight, you are mine, Jennie." Jennie gently pushed Perry's body back from hers. "I have the wagon ready for us, Perry", she whispered. Perry smiled as he turned to walk away. "We have a lot to do before we bed down, Jennie." I'll take care of the horses while you get a fire started. Woman, make us something to eat. I'll be having some of that whiskey I brought from Cherry Creek tonight". Perry jumped in the air, threw his hat high and caught it behind him. Shaking her head, Jennie pursed her dry lips and smiled. While Perry worked with the horses, Jennie returned to her wagon, tilted the heavy water jug and poured water into a metal bowl. Furtively, she closed the curtain, removed her heavy dress, and hurriedly washed her face and body. The water had warmed during the day in the ceramic jug. Although the water was to be saved for drinking, Jennie squandered it to revitalize her body for Perry. She brushed her hair, quickly braided her silky curls and drew her favorite white linen dress with hand stitched yellow embroidery from the pack. Jennie had never worn the dress. It was to be her "special occasion" dress. There hadn't been a special occasion for Jennie. Holding the dress to her bosom, she caressed the embroidery threads, remembering the weeks she spent working on the intricate needlepoint pattern. She remembered stitching late into the nights after Lizzy fell asleep. Perry had never seen the dress since it was secretly packed away after Lizzy died. Carefully unfolding the dress, Jennie slipped it over her head and smoothed the deeply formed creases with her hands. This was the only dress

Jennie owned that didn't have a high collar to conceal her neck. The neckline lunged deep in the front exposing a hint of her velvety pale breasts. Hearing Perry's clinking feed bucket outside the wagon, Jennie quickly removed the dress and hung it on a side peg. She slipped her dusty, lifeless dress back on and hurried to leave the wagon to prepare the meal for the evening. Curiously, Perry glanced at Jennie as she jumped off the wagon. "Is everything ok? Jennie?" Jennie lowered her eyes and said quietly "I'm fine, Perry. I was just tidying up a bit".

CHAPTER 26
A GOOD DIRT NIGHT

Every good meal began with boiling water. Jennie dug through the brown dusty burlap sack to retrieve a handful of small red potatoes. As the water boiled frantically, she dropped them into the charred black metal pot. Staring into the pot, she felt the warm steam wafting up to comfort her face and neck with soft pulses of moisture. She closed her eyes and drew the warm steam into her nostrils. It seemed an uncommon comfort to Jennie this night. The steam softened her cracked lips. She felt a surge of warmth move through her body as she leaned over the boiling water. Almost trance-like, she lingered in the stooped position. Shaken from the hypnotic moment, Jennie jumped and turned in anxious surprise when Perry touched her shoulder from behind. Grasping her arm, Perry blurted "Jennie, I am sorry to startle you. Can I help you with dinner?" Gathering her senses, Jennie shook her head and asked "Can you bring me some meat from the cold crock?" Perry returned to the campfire with meat tightly wrapped in yellow waxed muslin. When Jennie unfolded the meat she looked at Perry in surprise. "Perry, this is our best meat! Do you want to use this now?" Sheepishly grinning, Perry said "Tonight is as good as any, Jennie." Jennie's eyes glistened as she looked into Perry's face.

"Tonight we will have a feast," she whispered. Jennie rummaged through the wagon larder. She sensed the excitement of preparing a Christmas dinner. Retrieving fresh carrots, apples and a crock of honey, she hummed softly as she set about to prepare the special meal for her family. In the distance she listened to Perry whistling. Jenny imagined that this could indeed be a special night for the Duncan family, even if it wasn't Christmas.

Perry Duncan poured a generous portion of home brewed whiskey into a dented metal cup. The heavy alcohol scent of the whiskey filled the still air. Perched on a stump by the campfire, he rested his tattered boots on a rock, leaned his head back to face the evening sky, and listened as Jennie scuttled around camp preparing the meal. A rush of heat moved into his throat from the whiskey as he called out, "Jennie, come over here to me".

. Wiping her hands on her skirt, she turned toward Perry and sauntered toward him. When she reached his side, he took her hand and pulled her down to his level. Jennie looked around then knelt on the ground at Perry's side. He set his whiskey on the ground and took Jennie's head in his hands and kissed her lips passionately. Jennie, with eyes closed, swallowed hard. She lunged toward Perry for another taste of his warm whiskey sullied lips. Their bodies drew closer. Perry dropped to the ground next to Jennie and pushed her gently to the ground. For a brief moment they were lost in each other's grip until the hissing sound of water boiling over on the campfire disturbed their embrace. Jennie pulled herself up to her elbow and swung around to see the youngsters standing by the fire looking curiously at her and Perry. "I'm coming"! She cried out as she leapt to her feet. Perry chuckled at the sight of his young sons gawking his way. In a low whisper he said "Damn". Jennie looked back toward Perry with a smile as she pulled the steaming pot off the fire. She could feel his eyes watching the way she moved.

Except for the clanking of forks on metal dishes, dinner was quiet and lighthearted. The meal was eaten quickly by the Duncans. Young garden carrots, glazed with fresh honey and sweet cream butter glistened on their plates. The "good meat" was a tender treat on this special evening. Perry looked up from his plate to Jennie. She drew into his lustful examination. Her cheeks flushed as she lifted her eyes toward her husband's handsome face. Averting her glance away from Perry, she struggled to cool her thoughts. Perry grinned as he directed his attention to his sons. The subtle glances between their parents did not escape their watchful young eyes. This uncommon behavior between Perry and Jennie was palpable. Their mother Jennie had a tranquil look about her tonight. The harshness in her expression had increasingly diminished on this night. Her face glowed softly in the firelight tonight and her kind smile drew her children's attention. Such curious interaction between their parents never happened in Cherry Creek. So many things were changing for the Duncan boys now as they gathered around the campfire on the Wyoming prairie. The pungent fragrance of the dark rich bottom soil and their father's cup of aromatic whiskey filled the dusky night air around the fire. Scraping his shoe in the dark soil, Jesse looked up and asked his father "Is this good dirt, Pa? Perry responded, "This is good dirt, son."

Jennie busied herself with cleaning up the dishes and putting supplies in their places. Calling his boys to his side, Perry announced that it was time to prepare the wagon for the night's sleep. "Let's get your bedrolls ready for the night, sons". Without hesitation, Perry's sons climbed into the wagon and unfurled their bedrolls. They each had their favorite placement of the bedding. Jesse slept between his brothers.

Jennie halted her job of cleaning up camp and rushed to her wagon. She quickly brushed her hair, tore off her soiled long dress and slipped the never- worn linen dress over her head. She reached into a small wooden box hidden under the side board and took a tiny bottle of rose water from the box. Splashing a few drops onto her neck, she closed her eyes and savored the sweet scent she hadn't worn in years. She fluffed the feather bedding and jumped from the wagon.

Once the children were tucked into their bedrolls, Perry said good night to his sons. "Can we say good night to Ma? Vere called out. Surprised at the request, Perry called back "I'll get her". Perry came up behind Jennie and wrapped his arms around her waist in the dim light of the fading flames of the campfire. He whispered in her ear "Your children want to say good night, Jennie". She turned to face Perry with a puzzled look on her face. "Are they in their bedrolls already?" Perry gazed at Jennie's revealing white dress in astonishment. "You are more beautiful than ever, Jennie", he whispered breathlessly. He took her hand and led her back to the boy's wagon. He raised her up to the wagon seat. She poked her head through the opening in the canvas tarp. "Good night, children. Tomorrow we will get an early start and head for Sheridan. Get a good night's sleep." Vere quietly said "Ma, I am glad you are here with us." "I am too, Vere. I am too" she repeated. Jennie lingered for a moment looking at her children. It was nearly dark now and she could scarcely make out their faces. Backing away and closing the canvas curtain, Jennie placed her hand over her mouth to muffle a sob. "Good night little ones", she whispered.

Leaning quietly against the wagon, Perry listened to Jennie's interaction with her sons. She had not addressed them as her sons yet. He was troubled that Jennie couldn't call them her sons.

Jennie stepped down from the wagon seat into Perry's open arms. The moment her feet touched the ground, Perry lifted her and carried her to the campsite. Resting her head on his shoulder, she buried her face into his neck. His scent occupied her senses. Perry took her hand and led her to the wagon. Lifting her up, he followed behind. After pulling the canvas curtain closed, he cradled her head in his hands and put his lips to hers. Jennie dropped to her knees and pulled him down to her. She slowly lifted the white dress over her head exposing her soft pale body. Unwinding the twisted braid, she let her long brown hair drop over her shoulders like a wavy chestnut waterfall. Perry's hands trembled as he pulled his heavy shirt off over his head and dropped his trousers to the floor. Together they rolled over onto the warm feather bedding Jennie had carefully laid out. It was the night Jennie hoped would come again. Together they spent the night on the prairie in each other's arms. The night was warm. The crickets chirped in the grass as they made love.

Perry woke in the early dawn. Rolling to his back, Jennie's warmth emanated like the gentle heat from a waning campfire. He could hardly wait to start the day. His lovely Jennie's temperament seemed as it was before the death of Lizzy. Could it be that she had finally left Lizzy in Cherry Creek? He rose carefully from the frothy feathered mattress so as not to disturb his Jennie. Clutching his clothing, he quietly moved from his place. The wagon swayed as he stepped through the canvas curtain. Jennie slept soundly still.

Once outside the wagon Perry stretched as he surveyed the campsite. He noticed that Jennie had not packed everything away in her usual way. Glancing back to the wagon, he remembered that Jennie had hurriedly gone to the wagon to put on her white dress for him. He remembered the sensation of her soft bare skin next to his body. He could still taste the sweetness of her warm moist lips and the aroma of the rose water on her mellifluous neck.

His mind lingered on his night with Jennie as he went to gather feed from the other wagon for the horses. As he dropped the backboard of the wagon, he heard his children stirring in their bedrolls. He abruptly stopped and waited till the sounds of them moving ceased. Slowly, he lifted a bag of feed from the wagon and backed away. He wanted more quiet time by himself this morning.

As Perry walked around the wagon he saw Jennie had left the wagon and was standing near the horses. Sleepy eyed, she watched Perry as he effortlessly carried the heavy sack of feed toward her. When he reached her he dropped the sack to the ground and gently pulled her close to him. Closing his eyes, he wrapped himself around her, holding her tight against him. Enfolding her arms around his waist, Jennie rested her head on his chest as they stood quietly motionless together in the cool morning air.

Jennie lifted her face toward Perry and whispered "I didn't get things put away last night like I should have. I had other things on my mind." The corners of Perry's mouth turned up slightly as he responded, "And what was so important that you neglected your chores, young lady?" Jennie covered her mouth to muffle her laughter when Perry tickled her waist wildly.

Perry's wagon's canvas curtain jiggled open to reveal the Duncan brothers chuckling side by side. Their tousled little curly heads peeked around the curtain watching their parent's playful commotion. "Get yourselves dressed!" Perry called out. The curtain jerked closed and the wagon rocked raucously as the boys scrambled around inside.

Jennie entered her supply box and retrieved a bag of fresh-ly ground wheat flour. She hadn't made pancakes for her family since they left Cherry Creek. She called out "Jessica, ask Pa to get some bacon from the cold crock"! Jesse stood dumbstruck looking at his mother. "Ma, that isn't my name anymore," he blurted out to her. His chin quivered as he looked at his mother in surprise. "I'm sorry, Jesse", she whispered to him as she leaned down to his face. "It just slipped out. I wasn't paying attention", she said quietly.

Perry looked up from the feedbag contemplating the exchange between Jennie and Jesse. He felt a surge of anxiety fill his heart as he watched Jesse's face crinkle into tears. Walking to his son's side, he took his arm and turned his son to him. "Jesse, your Ma just made a mistake. Don't let this bother you". Jesse nodded his head and wiped the tears from his cheeks. "Pa, I don't want to be Jessica", he sobbed. Speechless, Perry hugged his young son. "Ma is making her special pancakes for us this morning. Let's see if she needs any help", Perry blurted out.

The light hearted mood of the morning abruptly dimmed after the incident between Jennie and Jesse. Perry approached Jennie as she quietly busied herself with breakfast. "Jennie, I know you didn't call Jesse by his former name on purpose. The boy is sensi-tive about being a young man now. We must try to remember this." Jennie, now somber faced, nodded in agreement, and glanced at Jesse standing alone by Perry's wagon. Desperately trying to recap-ture the bliss of the morning, Perry called to his sons to get ready for breakfast. "Get your bedrolls packed up sons! Ma's pancakes will be done soon."

Unaware of Jesse's mournful event, Ike and Vere scrambled into the wagon to pack their bedrolls before breakfast. Jesse followed behind. Perry walked to the side of the wagon and overheard Jesse relay the event to his brothers. "Ma called me Jessica this morning", he said. Vere replied, "She just forgot, Jesse. She just forgot one time." Wrestling with his bedroll, little Ike was too busy to join into the conversation. "She doesn't like my new name", Jesse replied in a cracking hushed voice. Vere answered, "She just forgot one time, Jesse. Don't be sad all day". Jesse yelled out "I'm never going to be Jessica again!" Perry jumped forward and called out to the boys to come out of the wagon and get ready for breakfast. "OK Jesse, that's enough. Come out now and help Ma get breakfast served." Jesse yelled out to Perry from inside the wagon, "I am not a girl who helps make breakfast, Pa." Vere and Ike jumped from the wagon leaving Jesse inside. Perry reached up and pulled the canvas curtain aside to see Jesse sitting inside on his bedroll. "Come out, son. You aren't going to be a girl just because you help your Ma. I help her out from time to time and I am not a girl." Jesse stepped outside the wagon and sat on the wooden seat with his hands on his hips and his lower lip protruding. Reaching up, Perry seized Jesse and pulled him to the ground. "We are finished with this talk now,

Jesse", he said quietly. Reaching down to take Jesse's hand, Perry was surprised when Jesse jerked his hand away from his father. Perry faintly grinned at his son's display of defiance. When Jesse walked as Jessica, hand holding was mysteriously acceptable. Today, and no day beyond this one, was going to be a hand-holding day for Jesse.

CHAPTER 27
CAUGHT IN THE RAPIDS

Pancakes on the prairie made Jesse a happier boy this morning. All the drama about Jennie calling him Jessica seemed to fade away with each bite of pancake soaked with sweet warm golden honey. Perry's voice held a tone of excitement as he relayed his plan to make it to Casper today. "Tonight we spend the night in Casper. We'll have some supper and see the town. Tomorrow we'll get supplies at the mercantile, buy some new clothes for you boys and start out for Sheridan". Jennie's eyes looked up from her plate at her sons as they listened to their father's plan for the day. Looking to his wife, he added, "We'll also find a new dress for Ma!" In unison, Jennie's boys turned their heads to their mother. Jennie smiled, shaking her head. "Your Pa has big plans for Casper, so we best be finishing breakfast and getting rigged up", she announced.

The wagons were packed and ready. Perry walked around each horse, patting their flanks as he inspected their feet. The boys loaded themselves into Perry's wagon. Jesse tapped his Pa on the shoulder from behind. "Pa, can I ride with Ma today?" he whispered. "Sure, son?" Jesse nodded. Dismounting the wagon, Perry reached up to bring Jesse to the ground. Once again Perry reached down to take Jesse's hand and once again Jesse pulled his hand away. They strolled together to Jennie's wagon. Jennie had been in the back of the wagon folding the bedding from the night before and startled when she saw Perry lift Jesse to the wooden seat. Perry called out to her "Ma, Jesse would like to ride with you to Casper". She ruffled the hair on Jesse's head and said "What are we waiting for, let's get going Jesse!" Jesse slid over on the seat to make room for his Ma to take the reins. Looking up to Jennie, he sat up tall as he could. "I'll help you find Casper, Ma", he proudly declared.

Perry's familiar sharp whistle sent the horses jumping forward. Jennie shook the reins and turned around to see Perry start his wagon moving at the same time. Jesse heard his Pa's voice cheerfully talking to his brothers from behind. Briefly he wished he was back with his Pa. His Pa would whistle a song and have his sons sing along. "Can we sing some songs, Ma?" Jennie looked down at her son's face and burst into a lively song. Surprised, Jesse eyed widened with wonder. He had never heard his mother sing. Jennie's voice filled the air with soft sweetness like Jesse had never experienced. His pink lips widened into a smile as he focused on his mother's voice. When she finished, Jesse told his Ma, "I like the song but I don't know that song, Ma. Pa sings railroad songs to us". "The name of that song I sang is THE WILLOW SWAYS IN THE WIND." Jennie told him. "Sing it again, Ma", he pleaded.

"The willow gently sways in the wind
On a sunny summer day.
I watch the graceful willow bend and dance the long sweet day.
And when the night time comes to be,
The willow waits and sleeps,
Until another sunny morning
Above the horizon creeps.

Jennie explained to Jesse that she learned the song when she was a young girl living in Pennsylvania. "My mother sang this song to me when I was around your age", Jennie said. Listening intently, Jesse watched his mother's eyes as she spoke about her own mother.

The trail to Casper veered off the flat prairie and followed the Platte River next to dense groves of cottonwood trees. High in the sky, the sun reflected off the limestone hills that dotted the terrain toward Casper. Around mid-day, Perry whistled to halt near the river in a grove of tall trees for a shady break. Guiding his team of horses to the bank of the river for cool water to drink, he signaled Jennie to do the same. After the horses drank, both wagons were driven back to the trail. Jennie prepared a simple lunch of dried meat and cheese for her family. After the meal the Duncan boys ran to the river's edge. Calling back to his parents, Jesse cupped his hands around his mouth and yelled "Can we go in the water?" Perry and Jennie looked to each other for the answer. Perry called back "Wait for me to join you!" By the time Perry reached the bank of the Platte, his boys had mostly undressed. "Let me go in first, sons. I'll check to see how deep the water is." Perry stripped down to naked and inched his way into the rocky river bottom. He signaled to his sons to come into the water with him. Jennie had approached closer to the river and gazed at her young sons and Perry as they sank into the lazy flowing water. She listened to squeals of delight echoing up from her sons as they splashed and jumped. The splashing water sparkled in the sunlight like tiny bursts of brilliant white light as it was flicked into the air. Perry called to Jennie "Ma, come in with us!" She shook her head and turned to walk back to the wagon. "Jennie! Come in!" Perry coaxed playfully. Turning back to the river, Jennie tilted her head, looked at her husband and pointed to her long skirt. Perry called to his sons, "Boys, it is time for you to get out and get dressed now." Howls of discontentment rose from his youngsters. "Now!" Perry yelled. The Duncan brothers hopped out of the water grabbed their clothes and ran up the embankment to the wagon.

Perry called again to Jennie to join him in the water. She looked back to the wagon where her sons were dressing. Jennie hid behind a stand of river willows and quickly disrobed. Out of sight of her children, she loped into the water and dove into Perry's outstretched arms. Together they swirled in the icy water. Jennie's long hair floated on the water as she twirled around with her arms locked around Perry's neck. Her cheeks were pink, her lips glistened in the noon sun and her eyes twinkled as a child. Perry lifted her in his arms and swam to the middle of the river with her. Locked in each other's arms, they blissfully drifted downstream without the realization that the water was moving much faster. Jennie was the first to notice that they had floated far downstream. Straining to stand up, she found the water too deep for her feet to touch bottom. In the next moment they were dragged apart in a section of rolling rapids with enormous boulders and a deep drop off over a dam- like formation plunging them into a dark icy whirlpool. Struggling to escape the grip of the powerful swirling current, Jennie's gurgling cries for help were muffled by the roar of the water tumbling over the slippery river rocks. Slamming her pale body against the rocks, the current gripped her mercilessly like sea serpent tentacles wrapping around her and pulling her deeper into the churning water. Hearing Perry's inaudible calls to her amid the turmoil, Jennie frantically searched the water for his face. Her stamina spent, she caught sight of him just as his hand gripped her weakened arm. Against the raging current, Perry drug Jennie to calmer water at the bank. Lying naked and breathless on the river bank, Perry cradled Jennie's trembling body against him. Their bruised and bleeding bodies shivered together.

Distant calls roused Jennie and Perry. The yells came louder and clearer. Their young sons had witnessed their parents being pulled away from them in the water. The panicked tone of their voices carried through the air. Stumbling to his feet, Perry stood and waved his arm to signal his location to his sons. Jennie managed to sit up wrapping her arms around her exposed body. Unflustered by their parent's bare bodies, the Duncan brothers tearfully clung to the legs of Perry and Jennie. Jessie sobbed out" We were afraid you drowned! " Kneeling on the ground, Perry securely gathered his sons in his arms. "Ma and I are fine now. Lead the way back to camp. Don't look back, just keep moving ahead and show us the way". Limping barefoot, naked Jennie and Perry clutched hands following their young sons along the riverbank without speaking. When they reached the place on the bank where their clothes were hung on willow branches, Perry told the boys to go to the wagon and get a blanket for their Ma. As Jennie was pulling clothes over her bruised body, Perry came to her and gently assisted her trembling hands. Her cheek and lip were swollen where she had been bashed against the rocks, her legs were scraped raw. He softly gathered her hair from her shoulders and pushed it to the back of her neck. Tenderly, he lifted her chin to him and said to her, "My darling Jennie, come up to camp and rest. I love you, Jennie". Jennie looked into Perry's eyes, covered her mouth and burst into raucous laughter. Astonished, Perry stepped back looking at Jennie. His eyes widened, then, he too buckled over in laughter. Leaning on each other, tears streamed down their cheeks as they roared in laughter.

Jennie and Perry hobbled up the river bank to their waiting sons. Standing at attention like little soldiers, the Duncan brothers' faces were frozen in confused contortions. Jesse stepped forward to hand a blanket to his Pa. The bewildered look on their sons' faces brought Perry and Jennie to hysterical laughter again.

Watching their parents with suspicion, the Duncan brothers sat quietly near the wagon. Jesse approached his mother tearfully "Are you okay, Ma?" Jennie knelt down in front of Jesse and said "Jesse, I am fine. The water was very deep and running fast in the middle and we were surprised how quickly it carried us downstream. Your Pa is a good swimmer and he rescued me. We won't let this happen again", she whispered.

Perry called to his children to get ready to get back into the wagons for making the last part of the trip to Casper. "Okay boys, let's get loaded and we'll get these wagons moving", he said. Jesse announced that he would be riding in the wagon with his Ma.

"Ma wants me to ride with her so I can help if she needs me", he proudly called back to Perry. Jennie looked surprised at Jesse's announcement since there hadn't been any discussion about him riding with her again. She looked at Perry and winked.

When the wagons were moving once again, Jesse softly said to his mother, "Maybe you could sing another song for me, Ma. I liked the one you sang about the willow tree." Jennie smiled down at Jesse and nodded. "I'll remember another one I'm sure", she said.

What was supposed to be a short break for lunch turned out to be much longer than expected for the Duncan family. "Swimming" in the Platte River was unplanned, yet exhilarating. Jennie's thick hair, still damp from the river water, formed tiny ringlet curls and framed her face beneath her bonnet. Her swollen cheeks blushed pink and purple. Seated next to his mother, Jesse noticed that her knuckles were scraped raw, as she grasped the reins. "I'm sad you hurt your hand in the river, Ma", he muttered. "Jesse, I told you I am fine!" she chortled. "If I was hurt bad, I wouldn't be driving this wagon!' Satisfied with his mother's reassurance, Jesse wiggled himself on the seat and faced forward.

CHAPTER 28
FIRST FISHING

The Duncan wagons maneuvered across the Platte River two more times during the afternoon as they pushed northward. Jennie followed the tracks where others had crossed without apparent incident. Dipping their noses and mouths into the water as they crossed, the horses took gulps of cool clear water. Jennie looked down into the river, remembering hers and Perry's last experience in the river. She twisted to look back at Perry's wagon with a smile on her face. Perry tipped his hat to his bride, seemingly knowing what her thoughts were at that moment.

Late afternoon sun sunk deeper into the hilly horizon. After the second river crossing, Perry whistled. Pulling her horse team to a halt, Jennie patted Jesse's knee and told him to stay seated. "I am going to talk to Pa for a minute. I'll be back", she said. As she turned to leave the wagon, Perry was already standing at the side of her wagon waiting. "We're not going to make it much further, Jennie. Casper is just too far away according to Augustine's map. How about we set up camp here next to the river and maybe take another swim?" Perry winked at Jennie as he turned to walk away. They pulled their wagons into a grove of tall willows at the curve of the river. Thick green underbrush grew at the bank of the river with a small beaten path formed from animals accessing the water.

The Duncan family gathered beneath the shade of the old willow branches. Perry instructed his sons to gather some firewood. While the boys were busy gathering wood and carrying it back to camp, Perry went to his wagon to retrieve two fishing rods with barbed wire hooks attached to sisal twine fishing line. "We're having fish for dinner." He called out. The boys came running to their father, reaching for the rods. Holding the rods above his head, Perry said, "Not so fast, sons. The first thing you need to do is dig up some worms or find some grasshoppers for bait." Jesse and Vere looked at each other curiously. They never dug worms in Cherry Creek. "Take this spade to the good dirt by the river and dig till you find some worms. Ike, you look for some grasshoppers". The three youngsters scurried off. Jennie observed her children rushing toward the river and called out. "Don't go in the water!" Jennie's admonition to her sons prompted Perry to haste to her. Whispering in her ear, he gripped her around the waist from behind saying, "Are we going for that swim later?" Jennie turned abruptly, facing Perry, she whispered, "In your dreams, Perry Duncan. I'm still stinging from our earlier swim." "Awe, come on Jennie, the water will do you some good. We'll wait till the boys go to bed." he hummed. Jennie snapped back, "In the dark, Perry? My God man, have you gone mad? We can't stay afloat in the daylight. What makes you think we can swim in the dark?" Perry clutched her shoulders, pulled her in, and kissed her forehead. "Jennie, you make me like a crazy man. You know that?" She pushed him away and responded, "You are a crazy man who needs to get this camp set up now. The horses need tended to."

Sprinting into camp with a dirty handful of writhing worms, Jesse beamed. Opening his hand to display his catch, he grinned with pride holding his open hand inches from Perry's face. Following behind him, Vere presented his cache of earthworms. Perry pondered that the adventure of finding the worms was perhaps more of an escapade than using them to catch fish.

"Where's Ike"? Jennie called out. Jesse and Vere looked around and shrugged their shoulders. Jumping to his feet, Perry ran toward the river. Jennie followed shouting Ike's name. When they arrived at the river bank, they frantically looked both directions in the water for their youngest son. There was no sign of Ike anywhere. Jesse and Vere arrived moments after their parent's at the river. Perry called out to his boys to search the thick willows around the area for their brother. "We didn't see him near the water, Pa. Ma told us not to go in the water", Jesse replied. Jennie's voice converted to a high tone. "Perry ! We have to find him! Oh my God, Iris, where are you?" Jesse and Vere stopped in their tracks and looked at their mother in horror. "Ma, his name is not Iris!" Jesse indignantly shouted back to her. Jennie stood speechless looking at her sons. "Find your brother now!" she yelled angrily.

Perry's voice called from far away downstream, "I found him!" Jennie tore through thick green willows that whipped her face wildly as she flung herself in the direction of Perry's voice. When she reached Perry, he was carrying Ike on his back. "I couldn't find any grasshoppers, Ma", he whimpered. Her face softened in relief as she looked into Ike's red watery eyes. Perry whispered, "We don't need any grasshoppers, Ike. Jesse and Vere found lots of worms. Let's go fishing now".

With only two fishing rods, the boys took turns holding the rods. Perry carefully splayed the worms on the barbed wire hooks and handed the rods to his sons. Sitting on the bank, Perry relished watching his boy's faces as they anticipated the first fish hit on the hook. Vere was calmly holding the rod when the first fish hit. It jerked the rod out of his hand. Jumping to his feet, Perry darted into the river to grasp the escaping rod. He reached into the water and grasped a large wiggling rainbow trout and brought it to shore. When Perry got the fish off the hook he handed the fish to Vere. Vere backed away in fright putting his hands behind his back. "No, Pa! I'm afraid!" he yelled. "It's okay, son. I'll take it to your Ma". As Perry walked to camp with the fish, he thought about his sons need for time to adjust to their new life as "boys". As he handed the fish to Jennie, more yelling came from the river and he quickly ran back. Jesse, holding on to his rod with all his might, grimaced as the rod jolted back and forth. Vere stood with his hands on his head as if to stay as far away as possible from the creature on the hook. "Hang on, son!" Perry laughed watching his oldest son conquer his first fish hit. "Help me, Pa!" Jesse blurted out. Perry waded into the river and acquired Jesse's fish from the hook and handed it to Jesse. Reluctantly, Jesse grasped the wiggling fish with both hands out in front of him as if to keep it as far away as possible. Both terrified and proud, Jesse carried his fish to camp. Jennie smiled when Jesse held it up for her to see. Just as he held it up high to his mother, the fish shot wildly from his hands and landed on the ground, flopping high in every direction. Fearfully, he backed away. Jennie softly told Jesse, "I'll take it from here, Jesse". "You are so brave, Ma", he looked up to his mother's face.

Thick summer warmth surrounded the Duncan camp site. Dusk settled in as the family devoured their fresh river catch. Gently gurgling over smooth rocks near the campsite, the Platte River softly lulled the family to mellow. Gazing at each other across the warm campfire, Perry and Jennie watched each other's eyes, anticipating a night in each other's arms. Frogs croaked and crickets chirped on the river bank as the Duncan boys prattled in a game of pick-up sticks next to the wagon.

As if on cue, a mob of bats fluttered out one by one from a woodpecker hole in the gnarled trunk of an old willow tree. As they swirled around the campsite, visible only by the yellow fire light, the sound of their whirring wings above the Duncan family brought shrieks from Jennie and her children. Perched on a stump near the campfire, Perry threw his head back in laughter, wrapping his arms around his stomach. "They are here to eat the mosquitoes!" he yelled, between bouts of hilarity. Abandoning their game of sticks, the Duncan boys sprinted to their wagon covering their curly haired heads. Jennie retreated to her wagon at the same time. "I'll clean the dishes in the morning", she yelled, peeking her head from the canvas wagon cover. Perry's deep laughter continued to echo through the river valley darkness.

CHAPTER 29

RIVER WILLOWS

As the chattering slowed from the Duncan boy's wagon, alone by the fire, Perry rose from his place and picked up a pot nearby. He strolled to the river's edge to fill the pot with water to extinguish the fire. As he was returning to camp, he heard the river willows rustling nearby. He stopped and stood motionless. Once again, the willows rustled, now louder and closer. He strained his eyes to discern any movement. Perry waited for more movement for a few minutes. When the rustling didn't happen again, he slowly walked to camp. The hot coals hissed like an angry snake as he poured the river water onto the flames. Without the campfire, the camp was in total darkness. Perry stood still in the blackness, waiting for any sounds coming from the willows. He found his way to the wagon and whispered to Jennie. "Jennie, find my gun and hand it to me". Jennie slowly pulled the canvas curtain open. She couldn't see Perry but could hear him breathing. "What is it, Perry?" There was an element of alarm in her whisper. He responded in a hushed voice, "It is probably a raccoon or skunk, Jennie. Something is moving through the willows near the river". Jennie felt her way to the inside wagon box and retrieved Perry's gun. She carefully handed the firearm out from behind the canvas and whispered, "Perry, here it is". Perry grasped the gun from her and leaned against the wagon facing the river. Suddenly, a loud thrashing sound came from the willows. Perry braced himself and aimed the gun in the direction of the noise. "Boys, are you in your wagon?' he bellowed. "We are, Pa", a faint voice called back to him. Jennie jumped in fright at the loud shout from Perry. "Stay there, do not come out!" Perry yelled back.

Jennie leaned through the open canvas and whispered "Perry, should I light a lantern for you?" A sliver of the moon had risen over the eastern horizon which was providing a dim light around the wagons. Jennie could make out Perry's apprehensive silhouette. His posture was that of a hunter aiming to kill. With the gun pointed toward the river he moved the gun back and forth from side to side. Keeping the gun raised, he slowly moved toward the space between the two wagons to provide coverage to his son's wagon as well. Jennie sat fixed in silence. Her hands were trembling as she felt around the pitch-dark wagon for her burlap wrapped weapon. Suddenly, the willows thrashed wildly again coming from two different directions. A thunderous gun blast pierced the silence. Perry's discharge into the darkness scattered the advancing menace to retreat downstream. The sounds of the willows snapping and swishing became more distant. Still aiming toward the river, Perry backed up to his son's wagon and called to the boys. "Everything is okay now, sons. There must have been a coyote or two in the bushes. They are gone now".

Perry knew it wasn't a coyote in the willows. He distinctly heard pounding of footsteps running down the river bank after the willows no longer were moving near the wagons.

"C'mon, sons, gather your bedrolls and come to your Ma's wagon for the night. I'll have your Ma light a lantern so you can get yourselves settled in for the night. We will all stay together tonight." Jennie heard Perry's instructions to the boys and lit the lantern quickly. Jumping down from the wagon, she carried the lantern to where Perry was standing. While the youngsters were gathering their bedrolls, she quietly pulled Perry aside and said "Perry, we both know that coyotes wouldn't make that much noise prowling through the willows. Something or someone is stalking us, Perry." Glancing into Jennie's face lit golden by the kerosene lantern, he whispered "I think it was a person or possibly more than one person. I heard footsteps running through the willows. It may mean that we are in tribal territory and have intruded into the tribe's space. We will leave here at first light and push north. We don't want to frighten the children but I think it is best that we stay in one wagon tonight. I will keep watch for the first few hours and have you watch for the next few. We just need to be together in case there is trouble." Nodding her head, she clenched her teeth, calling to her sons to hurry along.

Marching across the dimly lit campsite, the small Duncan boys dragged their bulky bedrolls to Jennie's wagon. Standing on the floorboard, Jennie reached down to clutch the bedrolls first, and then the child attached to each. Her sense of urgency to get the children into the wagon was evident to her children. "Ma, can the coyotes jump up and get us in the wagon", Jesse quietly asked. She responded, "No child, you will be safe in the wagon. Move your bedrolls as far to the back of the wagon as you can get. We'll be cozy in the wagon tonight. Crawl to the back and get your bedrolls set up. Pa is watching out for us." Anxiously rearranging supplies, Jennie's hands continued to tremble. Her thoughts took her back to her encounters with the Indians who confiscated Perry's gun on the prairie. She recalled the young Indian man who helped her. She recalled the shot in the dark that had never been revealed to Perry. Her mind battled with dreadful possibilities they could face in the dark night ahead. Lost in her thoughts she scarcely heard her young sons arguing over where to place their bedrolls for the night. Perry came to the side of the wagon, calling through the heavy canvas side, he instructed his sons to be quiet. Startled by Perry's unusually stern warning, the Duncan boys hushed.

After the boys were tucked into their beds, Jennie left the wagon to be at Perry's side. "This worries me, Jennie", he whispered. "We need to listen carefully for any movement in the willows or from the flatland behind us. I want you to put out the lantern so there is no light in camp. The darkness is obviously not a problem for whomever or whatever is out there. We are at a disadvantage since we aren't familiar with our surroundings. For all we know, we could be very close to a tribal camp. I should have scouted the area more carefully when we arrived. I am sorry this is happening to us, Jennie." Jennie took a deep breath, threw back her shoulders and responded to Perry with quiet force. "Listen to me Perry Duncan, we didn't intentionally invade anyone's territory here and we haven't done anything to intimidate. We will defend our family at any cost if there is trouble. You know I am a good shot. We will get through this night together." Perry wrapped his arm around Jennie's shoulder and held her tight against his side. "Try to get some rest, Jennie. I will stay outside here and keep a listen. If I need to rest, I'll let you know to replace me out here for a bit." Jennie grasped his arm then turned to get back into the wagon. She knew there would be no rest for either one of them tonight. Closing her eyes, she darkened the lantern.

CHAPTER 30

A GOOD PISTOL WHIPPING

Jennie listened for movement outside the wagon. The slight moon overhead generously radiated a dim grey light. Her eyes had adjusted just enough to the darkness that she could make out Perry's silhouette through the worn canvas curtain. She could see Perry turning his head from side to side leaning against the sideboard of the wagon. His jacket scraped against the weathered wood as he shifted his position. It was ghostly quiet now. Even the crickets and frogs hushed on the river bank. As the hours passed, Jennie's eyes grew heavy. She couldn't let herself sleep and leave Perry alone to face the darkness himself. The soft rhythmic breathing of the Duncan children comforted Jennie through the long night. Glad they had no understanding of what could be happening outside their warm cocoons, Jennie rested her head on the side of the wagon cover.

Sudden movement by Perry shattered the calm. He called out to her in a loud whisper. "Jennie, get your gun out!" Jennie's heart raced. She could feel the blood cursing through her temples. Grasping her gun, she threw the curtain aside and dove onto the wooden bench. "Perry, what is happening?" She breathlessly called to him. "We have company again, Jennie. There is something on the east and something on the west side of the wagon. You need to cover the east and I'll cover the west. The urgency in his voice sent chills to Jennie's body. Dawn was slightly breaking over the eastern horizon as her tired eyes strained to see movement. She slid her legs over the side of the seat and dropped to the ground bracing her hips against the wagon as she gripped her gun tightly in front of her. Memories of holding the gun in the darkness flooded in. This time was different. With her family at risk, she would shoot to kill anyone or anything that advanced in the murky light. Tied to a tag line to the south of the wagons, the horses shuffled restlessly and snorted. Perry's attention shifted to the horses. "They're after the horses, Jennie", he called out to her in a coarse whisper. Panicked, she called back "What should we do, Perry? "You stay by the wagon. I'll circle around to the horses." Moving slowly to the front of the wagon, Jennie's arms quivered as she struggled to steady her gun in front of her. Suddenly, a noise at her side broke her grip as she swung the heavy gun wildly in the direction of the noise. The forceful swing hit something square on. A loud guttural groan reverberated through the darkened camp and a heavy body hit the ground with a thud. In the dim light, she could see that a man lay at her feet motionless. From a distance, Perry called out to her "Jennie, are you okay?" She answered back, "Perry I need you here." She heard his heavy footsteps running in her direction. When he got to her, he pulled her away from her stance above the man on the ground. "Get me some rope, Jennie." Jennie stumbled back to the sideboard of the wagon and grasped a rolled up line of rope. "Get your gun, Jennie and watch the horses", his coarse voice called to her. Jennie snatched her gun from the ground and walked crouched bent knees toward the horses. She could feel the adrenalin surging through her body. Her sight and sense of hearing was heightened.

Kneeling on the ground next to the limp body, Perry flipped the man over, pulled his arms behind his back and tied his arms and legs together as he had done many times in calf roping. When he flipped the man's body back over, he noted the man's face was bloody from a large gash above his eye. The man was an Indian dressed in hide leggings and tunic. Sucking in a long breath, Perry rose to his feet and turned to find Jennie. As he stepped forward, his foot struck something metal. It was a rifle. He grabbed the rifle and ran towards the horses.

Still crouching close to the ground, Jennie turned as Perry came closer. "It's me Jennie!" She whispered, "Perry, I don't think there is anyone here. The horses have settled down." Side by side they backed up toward the wagon scanning the area around camp. The sky was light enough to see each other's faces. Perry turned to Jennie. "Jennie, I am in constant admiration of you. How did you manage to take down that warrior without shooting him and rousing the whole valley? She smiled and shrugged her shoulders. "Well, I got his gun so we are safe from him for now. We need to get rigged up and get out of here. Jennie walked over to the man on the ground and looked carefully at him. "What about the man on the ground, Perry?" "He isn't going anywhere, Jennie. We will leave him for his friends to find him. I know he wasn't alone. There was another warrior with him. We aren't going to wait around for him to get back here".

As quietly as possible, Perry and Jennie set about getting the horses rigged back to the wagons. Jennie quickly gathered the dishes and pots and stacked them in the wagon box to be cleaned at the next camp stop. Through all the activity, the small Duncan boys stayed asleep warm in their bedrolls. When Jennie seated herself to move the wagon, the children stirred. Jesse called from deep inside the wagon, "Why are we leaving now, Ma?" Jennie put her finger over her lip to hush the child. "Stay back there for now, Jesse. Tell your brothers to stay in the back as well". With her gun parked on the seat next to her, Jennie signaled her team to move forward. As she pulled away, she looked down at the Indian man tied on the ground. His eyes were still closed and he hadn't moved since Perry had tied him. There was something about the man's face, besides the deep bloody gash, that troubled her.

Perry followed behind.

The wagons moved swiftly across the prairie that morning. Perry and Jennie kept their eyes moving, watching hillsides, looking in every direction for any sign of movement. High in the sky now, the sun was warming the summer air quickly as they rushed their horse teams faster than ever before. As they approached the next crossing of the Platte River, Perry signaled a halt. Dismounting his wagon, he had the Indian's rifle in his hand. He walked up to Jennie's wagon, stood silently at the side of the wagon, and held the gun up for Jennie to see. "Jennie, do your recognize this gun?" Jennie's eyes grew wide as she examined the gun. "My God, Perry that is your gun! That is the gun that was taken from me. Oh my God, Perry. That man would surely have killed me." she whispered to Perry. "He would have killed me the day he took it if it wasn't for the .." Perry looked at her and said "If it wasn't for what?", he asked. "If it wasn't for the young Indian man who was with him", she added. "It is a long story, Perry. The young warrior with the older Indian man who took the gun wouldn't let him kill me. I owe my life to that young man. We also owe our son's life to him as well. His mother was the woman who brought the snake bite medicine to Catherine. The story is long and complicated. Just trust me that the man who took the gun from me is laying tied up on the ground back at the campsite". "Well, I guess you got even with him, Jennie." Turning away, Perry's eyes softened as he grinned back at Jennie. "I'll be anxious to hear the rest of the story, Jennie. For now we need to get some food into these young ones and get back on the trail. We aren't out of reach yet. By now the tribe may have found our captive back at camp." Jennie turned on her seat and looked back to the trail. "Maybe we should just keep going, Perry. I can give the children something to eat as we move." Perry responded, "I'm hungry as hell, woman. We all need to get something to eat before pushing on. That includes you, Jennie."

Lunch consisted of dried meat, dehydrated fruit and cheese. After consuming the food, Jesse asked if they could go down by the river and play for a while. Jennie scolded "No, you cannot go to the river. We need to get back on the trail and move north to Casper." Jennie's boys dropped their heads. "Ma, we haven't been out of the wagon for a long time", Jesse blurted out. Perry said quietly, "That is enough, son. Your Ma is right. We need to get to Casper to get supplies. When we get to Casper you will have time to play." Jennie and Perry glanced at the trail behind them. Unaware of their parents worry, the Duncan boys shuffled in their seats.

CHAPTER 31

CROSSING THE RIVER

Perry moved ahead of Jennie's wagon to cross the river first. His wagon tilted and creaked as he trekked across. When he reached the other side, he dismounted and stood at the bank while Jennie crossed. Tentatively, her team stopped mid-stream. She grasped the whip hanging by the side of the wagon and sent a sharp crack to their backs. The horses lunged forward tipping the wagon to near tilting point. Perry jumped into the river to wade out far enough to grab a harness. His foot slipped on a rock as he treaded across the rushing Platte River. Soaking wet, he surfaced and was able to get the harness in his hands. Guiding the horse team across the river, he saw his young sons panic stricken peering from the back of the wagon. With a wide smile on his gleaming wet face, he called out "I'm okay, boys. These clothes needed a good rinsing."

Reunited on the other side of the river, the family stood together as Perry removed his dripping wet shirt and wrung the water from it. Perry scanned the horizon to their backs and said loudly, "Get back in your wagon now. Let's get moving, Jennie," he said as he blinked toward the horizon. Jennie turned to see a horse with a rider standing on a far off ridge overlooking the river where they had crossed. She could see the tail of the horse swishing in the breeze. Without a moment delay she lifted young Ike onto the wagon and nudged the others to get into the wagon. Perry motioned for Jennie to lead the way. She cracked the whip again to move her team quickly forward.

Fort Casper was their next stop. Perry relentlessly looked back behind his wagon to see if they were being followed. He nervously shifted on his seat as the horses pushed forward. Jennie drove her team fast and hard, looking back occasionally. Her face was creased in concern. Perry needed to get his family to Fort Casper for protection from tribal retaliation for tying up one of the warriors at camp. Steep hills slackened them as they traveled closer to Fort Casper. It was late afternoon as they moved over the last high ridge overlooking Fort Casper. Tiny primitive log homes dotted the hillsides near the Platte River. Jennie let up driving her team hard as they approached the small Wyoming outpost. A grass covered mountain range cast a cool shadow over Fort Casper in the evening. As she grew closer to Fort Casper, Jennie's shoulders relaxed. Following close behind, Perry felt a sense of relief wash over his tired body. The rest of the trip was downhill. Nevertheless, the horses were spent.

CHAPTER 32

CASPER, WYOMING

Dust swirled around the dirty streets of Fort Casper. Tied up in front of every building in the busy town, horses shifted from one foot to the other as Perry and Jennie pulled through town. Men in battered chaps and contorted hats hurried along the wooden boardwalks, nodding their heads and tipping their hats as Jennie passed by. The Duncan boys lined up behind Jennie's seat watching in wonder at all the activity of the busy town. "Pa is going to buy us some new clothes here", Jesse yelled out to Jennie from behind. With a smirk on her face, Jennie looked back to Jesse. "I will make you more clothing, darling Jessica." She muttered quietly to herself.

Jennie parked her wagon at the end of the street. "I've got to find some water for these horses. Stay here and I'll be back. Don't leave the wagon. Do you hear me"? She quickly disappeared into the Mercantile two doors down. Minutes later Perry pulled his wagon in beside Jennie's. He jumped down and looked into Jennie's wagon to see the Duncan boys sitting quietly. "Ma said we have to wait till she gets back, Pa. When can you buy us new clothes?" Perry's eyes sparkled with eagerness as he jumped up on the seat of the wagon. "As soon as your Ma gets back we all will go shopping for supplies and some new clothes. Where did your Ma go?' Vere piped up, "She went to get water for the horses." Puzzled by Vere's response, Perry looked around for Jennie. "It's okay, we'll wait for Ma. She'll be back soon." Perry whispered.

When Jennie returned to the wagon, she looked up to Perry on the seat. She was holding a package wrapped in burlap. "We made it to Fort Casper, Perry", she smiled. Without any mention of what her package was, she slipped it into the wagon box. "What do you say we get something to eat? Perry bellowed. "I saw an eating establishment down the street that serves home cooked meals. We could all use some food about now." Jennie blurted out, "But Perry, I can make dinner for us when we find a place to camp." "Not tonight Jennie. Tonight someone is going to cook for you." He jumped down from the wagon. Pinching her cheek, he brushed the hair from her face and winked.

The Duncan boys had never had a meal outside of their parent's home or campsite. When they walked into the Riverside Café, they were spellbound by the noisy atmosphere and number of people milling around. The pungent smell of fried bacon filled the smoky room. Spaced closely together, the roughhewn tables were covered with faded table cloths. Every table in the café was occupied with revelers. The only empty seats were at the large wooden bar at the back of the café with tall bar stools. Jennie turned to leave the building. At that moment a boisterous tousled haired redhead woman strolled up to the family and asked if she could help them. Perry said cheerfully "Yes Mam. We want to get some food to eat". She looked around the room and yelled to the bartender, "Any space back there for these hungry folks, Jake?" He signaled yes. "Follow me folks, there's a table back by the bar." "I don't think that will work for us Mam". Jennie called out to her as she walked away. "Sure it will Jennie, follow the lady," Perry said. Jennie cast a disapproving look toward Perry as he nudged his timid sons forward. "Get yourselves seated and I'll be back to take your order. All we have left now is some meatloaf and smashed potatoes. Can I get you a whiskey, Mister?" "Yes you can, Mam", Perry looked around and nodded his head. "Yes you can".

Perry Duncan sat high in his chair watching the circus of goings on in the Riverside Café. "This is mighty fine whiskey you have here, Mam. You can bring me another when you get a chance." "Comin up Mister", the red-haired woman yelled back. Jennie looked strong at Perry and shook her head. The small Duncan boys nervously watched their mother's face turning stern. Perry smiled as the food arrived and was placed in front of his children. "Mind your manners, sons. Jennie, you do the same." Perry chortled.

With the whiskey and the dinner finished, the Duncan's took to the door. Perry's old boots clomped on the wooden floor as they strolled past the tables of chattering patrons. The red-haired woman yelled from the back of the room to them them "Thanks folks, come back soon." Jennie never looked back. She never looked around the room once. Straight –faced, she ushered the Duncan boys out the door. When they were outside Jennie pulled Perry's arm to her side and said, "This is no place for these youngsters, Perry. We won't be coming back here or any place like this. You hear?" "Well I do hear ya, Mam. C'mon Jennie, can't we have a little fun once in a while? These boys need to see what the real world is all about", Perry swayed as he spoke.

As they walked back to the wagons, Perry told Jennie to take the boys ahead while he stopped into the Mercantile. When he got inside, he searched the store for children's clothing and found new britches and shirts for his sons. Holding up the clothing to determine sizes, he chose three long sleeve cotton shirts and three pair of dungarees for his boys. As he walked to the front of the store he saw a wooden mannequin clothed in a woman's blue dress with satin ribbon trim. He stood in front of the dress lost in thought of how his lovely Jennie would look in a dress the color of her light blue eyes. Reaching deep in his pocket, he retrieved his calfskin pouch with heavy silver and gold coins. Counting his coins, he realized that his purchase would leave the pouch nearly empty. Perry stared at the stack of new clothing in his arms, then to the blue dress. As he reached the counter to pay for the new clothes, he asked the man at the counter to get the blue dress from the mannequin. After the dress was brought to the counter, he asked that it be wrapped separately from the children's clothing. After the new items were wrapped, he asked where he could put up the wagons for the night. "I don't want to get too far out of town. We had some problems with Indians on the way here from Cheyenne", he said quietly. The man at the counter told Perry there was some good camp space near the river just west of town. He added "Mister, we have some Indians who trade here at the Mercantile from time to time. We haven't had problems with them. You must have gotten yourself into some tribal territory along the way." Gripping the packages, Perry tipped his hat and left the building.

When Perry arrived back at the wagons, Jennie had the Duncan boys settled into her wagon. She was seated on the wagon with reins in her hands. "We are ready to go, Perry", she said tersely. Shaking his head grinning, Perry climbed onto his rig with his package tied with twine and pushed forward. He steered his wagon around Jennie's down a back road south of the Main Street. As they ambled down the rutted grimy road, Jennie noticed a horse with red feathers woven into its mane. The horse was tied up to an old wooden post on the edge of town. The building in front of the post had a weathered sign "FORT CASPER DISPENSARY". She jerked the reins and stopped the wagon abruptly. Staring at the horse, she caught her breath. "Why are you stopping, Ma", Jesse called out to her from inside the wagon. "No reason, Jesse. Just looking around", she said slowly. Jennie pushed her wagon ahead, looking back until the horse was no longer visible.

Jennie's mind raced with possible reasons for the red feathered horse to be in Casper this day. Was it customary to have red feathers woven into horses' manes in Wyoming and was there was more than one horse with red feathers? Was the young Indian man with the red- feathered horse in Casper? If so, why was his horse tied up in front of the dispensary? Was he hurt or was he with someone who had been hurt? "Aha", she said to herself. "Did he bring the older Indian man to the dispensary who had been cold cocked with her gun at the campsite?' She had half a mind to turn the wagon around and enter the dispensary herself to find out if the horse belonged to the young Indian man who helped her so many times on the prairie. But then, what if he was with the injured Indian man who had Perry's gun and recognized her? Jennie shook the reins and pushed her team forward. Unaware of the mental turmoil Jennie found herself engrossed in, perched high on his wagon, Perry whistled his way down the dusty road bound for a long- awaited Casper campsite. The wind carried snippets of his whistling as she followed behind.

Whipping her hair as she moved her wagon along toward the campsite for the night, the robust Casper wind blew sheets of dust from Perry's moving wagon against Jennie's parched face. Her eyes burned hot and red from the intense sun of the day. As the sun sank deeper over the west, the road seemed less formidable. It was a road less traveled and smoother ride. Jennie left the red-feathered horse in Casper as well as its possible young Indian rider. The process of leaving behind her precious Lizzy in Cherry Creek and the young Indian man in Casper felt akin to Jennie tonight. Their presence was with her but felt less burdensome as she got closer to Sheridan. Tonight they would sleep in friendly territory; she closed her eyes and sucked in a deep breath as her team of horses followed closely behind Perry's wagon.

Perry pulled his wagon into a shaded flat area not far from the river. A tall cottonwood tree provided a leafed canopy over the wagon. Before dismounting, he stood tall on his seat and scrutinized the area. From his vantage point, he searched the entire area for anyone or anything out of the ordinary. He was careful not to park the wagon as close to the river as he had the night before. He had made sure to have a defensible space around him this night, even though the man at the Mercantile had told him they would be safe in the Casper area.

Jennie pulled her wagon close to Perry's and halted the horses. She too stood high on her seat and perused the area. Restlessly, the Duncan boys were lined up behind the seat waiting for Jennie to give permission for them to exit. When she motioned to them to leave the wagon, they leaped off the side of the wagon with their arms over their heads as if winging to freedom.

Perry approached them with a wide grin on his face. "How about a short swim while there is still some light?" he said. Turning to Jennie he yelled, "I'm talking to you too, young lady!" "I'm too tired right now, Perry. I would probably float on down the river before you could catch me, she called back. I will get the bedrolls set up and get things in order while you take a swim." The Duncan boys wasted no time stripping off their baggy clothes, each leaving theirs in a crumpled pile on the river bank. "Whoa boys, Perry called out to them. Let me go in first to make sure it isn't too fast or deep for you." Hopping on the bank of the river, Perry's boys kicked at the water waiting for Perry to reach them. Perry stripped his clothes off and walked slowly into the water. The bottom of the river was soft cool mud. Ankle deep, the water slowly gurgled over the smooth white rocks beyond the bank. "C'mon in boys, Perry called out. One by one, the Duncan boys sank into the cool river water. Splashing and kicking, their happy voices carried to Jennie's ears as she busied herself with the wagons.

Jennie organized her wagon putting things back to their proper spaces. She noticed the dishes stacked hastily in a canvas sack from the night before that needed to be cleaned. As she was about to leave the wagon, she reached deep into the storage box and pulled out her package wrapped in burlap. Untying the twine, she lifted a piece of folded pink flowered cotton muslin. Holding it to her bosom, she closed her eyes and rocked back and forth for a moment. Hearing Perry's voice calling to her from the river, she quickly wrapped the fabric, tied the twine tightly around it and returned it back to its hiding place.

Clutching the sack of soiled dishes, she jumped from the wagon and grabbed a tin bucket from the side board. Jennie slowly walked toward the river swinging the bucket as she strolled. As she reached the bank of the river, Perry surfaced and called out to her. "Jennie, please come in the water with us." The Duncan boys' heads turned to see their mother's response. "I'm going to get the dishes washed for tomorrow's breakfast, Perry," she called back. As she dipped the bucket in the river, Perry swooped up two handfuls of river water and flung it toward Jennie, soaking her to the waist. Jennie heaved the bucket of water into the river in response. As Perry retrieved the bucket and waded to the shore, he calmly handed the bucket back to Jennie. As she reached for the bucket handle, Perry grabbed her arm and pulled her into the river. Dumbstruck, the Duncan boys gasped in disbelief at their father's actions. When Jennie surfaced, her hair covered her face. Choking on the cold river water, she pushed the hair from her face, looked at Perry in disbelief. "My God, Perry. What are you thinking? My clothes are soaked now! They will never be dry for morning", she shrieked. He responded with a sheepish grin, "My darling, you worry needlessly." As Jennie stood in chest deep water, her skirt floated to the top of the water like a drifting water lily. Jennie's sons came to her side and stood motionless. Jennie looked at their anxious faces and burst into laughter. With water dripping from her eyelashes, she cried out to her sons, "Don't you go acting like your father, you hear me"! Treading water at a distance, Perry howled in laughter after hearing Jennie's orders to the Duncan boys. Dragging her long heavy wet skirt behind her, Jennie lumbered to shore. Turning back to the river she yelled "And now my shoes are wet as well, Perry Duncan. I suppose I shouldn't worry needlessly about that too!"

Perry watched as Jennie clutched her skirt attempting to wring out the water at the shore line. Gathering the long skirt in her hands, she held it high to keep it from dragging on the dusty ground. Exposing her pale slender legs, she disappeared behind her wagon. "Let's get out of the water and give your Ma some help back at camp", Perry ordered. After his sons were on shore, grabbing his clothes, Perry paced stark naked to the wagon to check on Jennie. She was perched on the wagon seat in her knickers and under shirt. Her wet skirt hung off the side of the wagon dripping water into a small puddle on the ground. "Lucky for you, I had dry knickers to put on, Perry Duncan", she hissed. "I wouldn't exactly call that lucky, Jennie", he chortled. He scooted up beside her on the seat, took her head in his hands and gently kissed her forehead. "Jennie, we'll be in Sheridan in a couple of days. Everything is going to be okay. Wait here and I'll be right back." Hopping on the ground next to Jennie's wagon, Perry managed to get his britches on over his wet legs before sprinting to his wagon.

Returning to Jennie's wagon, Perry leapt onto the footboard and handed her the package with the new blue dress folded neatly inside. As she untied the burlap bundle, she looked up curiously at Perry. Her eyes widened as she lifted the crisp linen dress by the shoulders. "What have you done, Perry? We can't afford this." Perry pinched her chin. "It is done, Jennie. Now put on the dress." Walking slowly to the wagon, she climbed inside, held the dress up, turned it around and nestled it to her face. Sniffing the fresh linen, she closed her eyes recalling her mother's love of linen. Lifting her blouse over her head, she cast it aside and dropped the fusty knickers from her waist. Judiciously, she slithered the delicate dress over her head. As it rested on her shoulders, she smoothed it over her breasts and hips. Standing alone in the wagon, she threw her head back and twirled around with her arms raised high.

A flurry of commotion outside brought Jennie to her senses. Pushing the curtain aside she watched her sons busily putting on their new clothes next to Perry's wagon. Jumping off the wagon, a wave of nausea came upon her as she steadied her stance. Closing her eyes again, she leaned back against the side of the wagon. "Jennie, you look beautiful", Perry hummed in her ear from behind. "I knew the dress was meant for you. It's the color of your eyes", he said quietly. Jennie turned to him and buried her face in his bare chest. "You flatter me, Perry Duncan. Any woman would look beautiful in this dress. Thank you for thinking of me. I love you, Mr. Duncan", she whispered.

Perry hadn't heard those words from Jennie since before Lizzy died in Cherry Creek. His eyes filled with tears as he rested his chin on the top of Jennie's head. "Jennie, you are my love. I would give you the world if it was mine to give. These past weeks have been a hard trip but we are getting close to Sheridan where we'll have a new life. Colorado is behind us now. Let's go check on those boys in their new clothes. "

As Jennie pulled away from Perry, she smoothed the creases on the dress. Noticing that it was a bit snugger around her waist than her old dress, she tried to adjust it and pondered that she never had a blue dress to wear. She never had a dress that matched the color of her eyes.

"Look, Ma, even our shirts have pockets"! Jesse yelled out as Jennie approached her sons. All three of the boys had their hands shoved into their breast pockets to show their Ma. Perry grinned as he watched his sons approving their new clothes and all the intricacies of their new oversized britches. "We'll have to roll up the britches for a while, boys. These will have to work for you. You'll grow into them before long. Don't you all look dapper in those new clothes?" he called out to them with a wide grin. "Ma, you look so beautiful in your new dress too", Jesse looked at his Ma with tender eyes. "Pa, did you get some new clothes too? Vere asked in a hushed voice. "I'll be getting my new clothes in Sheridan," Perry replied cheerfully. Jennie turned to Perry and smiled. "Pa looks handsome even in his old clothes, "she whispered.

"It's getting darker outside now so let's get camp set up for the night." Perry called out in a military type voice. "Boys, you need to gather some firewood." "Pa, should we put on our old clothes to get firewood?" Jesse questioned. "No, son. You can wear your new clothes to get firewood". Perry answered with a grin. The proud Duncan boys cautiously toted firewood back to camp wearing their new clothes.

Jennie hadn't gotten the dishes washed after the river incident. She said to Perry. "I won't be washing dishes in this dress, Perry. I don't care what you say. I will wash them tomorrow morning before breakfast and we won't be taking any swims before breakfast. You hear me?" Perry was quick to answer "I hear you, woman."

The evening cooled nippily on the Casper prairie. Winds from the northwest chilled the campsite near the river so much that the Duncan boys were anxious to crawl into their bedrolls shortly after sunset. Perry and Jennie sat wrapped in their oiled canvas coats near the fire talking about the trip ahead of them. "Tomorrow we head directly north, Jennie. A ways up toward Sheridan we will have to cross the Powder River which is a wide stream but not so deep according to Augustine's directions. There are a few other smaller streams to cross after the Powder River but Augustine said they wouldn't be a problem unless there was a heavy rainfall in the Big Horn Mountains. A small outpost south of Sheridan called Buffalo will be our third night stop. Fort Fetterman is nearby so we should be safe there. We will start getting into Indian Territory north of Buffalo and Fort Kearney, so we will need to keep an eye out near Buffalo. We should be able to get to Sheridan in a day or so after we leave Buffalo if the weather and the horses hold out. We'll keep our guns close on this leg of the trip but hopefully we won't need them."

By the fire, Jennie sat with her legs pulled up under her new blue dress and her coat pulled up over her chin as the cold Casper wind whipped the tree branches above them. "I'm ready to get into the wagon, Perry. I'll check on the children while you put the fire out."

When Jennie reached the boy's wagon, she noticed that their new clothes were neatly folded in three stacks on the seat. She called up to the children "Good night children. Are you all settled in now?" There was no response. She climbed onto the sideboard and peeked around the curtain to see that the Duncan boys were sound asleep in their bedrolls. As she rested on the seat next to the stacks of clothing, she whispered, "Good night, Jessica. Good night, Vera. Good night Iris."

Perry's voice startled Jennie as she sat quietly on the seat. "Jennie, the fire is out now and I have the wagon ready for us. Come on down now. The boys will be safe tonight." He reached up for Jennie's hand as she stepped down from the seat. He held her hand tightly as they walked to their wagon. Before climbing up, Perry slid the heavy coat off Jennie's shoulders. "Let me look at you one more time tonight in the blue dress, Jennie. You are the most beautiful woman in Wyoming tonight, Jennie". She gently pushed his hand away. "Stop it, Perry Duncan. You are making me feel like a silly school girl in her Sunday dress." "Well, in that case, Jennie, let's get into the wagon. I'll be the teacher and learn you a thing or two." Pulling her in close, he pressed his lips hard against Jennie's. His hands tracked the curves of her body as he lifted her onto the wagon. "I will remember this night in Wyoming, Jennie." He grasped the blue dress and carefully lifted it over Jennie's head. Her thick wavy hair flooded onto her bare shoulders in torrents as she fell backwards onto the bedrolls. The Duncan wagon swayed in a slow deep rhythm as the Casper wind fluttered the canvas walls in the dark. "You make me crazy fast, woman", Perry spoke breathlessly.

A ruckus outside the wagon woke Jennie from a deep sleep. She lifted herself to her knees to listen more carefully. Jabbing Perry in the side, she whispered "Perry, wake up". Perry sat up, brushed his hair from his face confused. "What, Jennie, what?" She whispered, "Something is happening outside". "Get your gun, Jennie.

Wait here. I'll check it out." Perry slowly pulled the curtain aside. All he could see was darkness. "What did you hear, Jennie?' he whispered. "I don't know what it was, Perry. It just woke me." A shrill guttural scream jolted the silence. "Jennie, it's a mountain lion", Perry yelled. He jumped to his feet and threw the curtain open yelling loudly "OUT!" The sound of heavy paws thumping the ground signaled the cat running from camp. A voice called from Perry's wagon "Pa, I'm scared"! "Light the lantern, Jennie. I'll go check on the boys." Jennie flicked a match filling the wagon with the smell of Sulphur. She lit the lantern and handed it to Perry who had already jumped off the wagon.

"Nothing to worry about, sons. It was a mountain cat prowling around camp looking for food. He is gone now and won't be coming back." "Can we get up now, Pa?' Perry looked to the east and saw that there was a thin streak of light just over the hills. "I guess it is about morning. Since we are all awake, I guess we can get moving early. An hour in the morning is worth two in the afternoon. I'll see if your Ma wants to get up."

Traipsing back to Jennie's wagon, Perry called out softly, "Jennie, are you awake?" She pulled the curtain aside. "I'm dressed for the day, Perry. The bedrolls are folded. We may as well get up and start breakfast", she said languidly. "I guess I would rather be woken by a mountain cat than angry Indians", she added.

Perry called out to his boys to pack their bedrolls and get dressed. One by one, they emerged from their wagon in their underwear. "Can we wear our new clothes, Pa?' "Yes, Jesse, put on your new clothes", he called back.

CHAPTER 33
OATMEAL FOR ORPHANS

"I need a cup of strong coffee this morning Jennie. I'll get some water from the river and get a fire going. I'm not sure we should be cooking any bacon this morning with the cat around. I'll get extra water and we'll boil up some oatmeal".

Jesse called out to his father. "We hate oatmeal, Pa." "Sorry son, today you get oatmeal for breakfast." "But Pa, Jesse yammered, "oatmeal is for orphans". That's what Aunt Elizabeth told us." Perry answered, "Aunt Elizabeth has never had your Ma's oatmeal and Aunt Elizabeth was never an orphan", Perry insisted.

Jennie emerged from her wagon in her new blue dress. She walked around to the side of the wagon where old her dress was hung to dry from the river dunk the night before. Still damp, she shook the dress like an old dusty rug and carried it back into the wagon. When she emerged the second time, she was wearing the old dress. Returning from the river with a bucket of water, Perry teased. "Not wearing your Sunday dress, school girl?" he said with a wink.

Bubbling oatmeal spurted high from the dented pot over the fire. The Duncan boys watched as it spilled into the fire hissing as it touched the flame. "What else can we have to eat Ma? Jesse murmured. "We'll put some dried cherries and honey on it", Perry announced. "C'mon boys, let's get this breakfast eaten so we can get going to Sheridan", Perry piped up.

Jennie hardly ate a bite of the oatmeal. She jumped up from her place and started picking up around camp. "Aren't you hungry, Jennie" Perry asked. "I ate some of the dried fruit earlier" she replied. Something about Jennie's behavior was troubling to Perry. He kept watching her as she puttered around the camp. She seemed listless, like she had no energy. Finishing his oatmeal, Perry got up and approached Jennie. He took her by the arm and pulled her gently aside. "Are you feeling okay, Jennie? You don't seem to be yourself this morning. The boys and I will take the dishes to the river and get them cleaned up this morning. Is there something else we can do?"

"I didn't get much sleep last night, Perry. I know we are in a safer place right now but I know we will have to go through some Indian territorial areas north of here and I just want things to go well. That's all. I just want things to go well for us". Perry wrapped Jennie in his arms and held her tightly. "We will be fine, Jennie Duncan. Don't go worrying on me now. The worst is behind us, you'll see".

Perry and the Duncan boys scuttled down to the river carrying all the breakfast utensils. Jennie could hear the clanking of the metal pots and dishes as they chattered. Leaning against one of the horses, she felt a wave of nausea go through her body again. She took a deep breath, brushed her hair back and slapped her cheeks. "Wake up, Jennie. This is no time to get squeamish", she whispered to herself.

The oatmeal crusted dishes were washed, the wagons were loaded and the Duncans prepared to push forward to Sheridan. Jennie suggested that the Duncan boys ride with their father for this leg of the trip. "Maybe the boys would like to ride with you for a bit, Perry. It would be good for them to have a change. This has been a long trip. I would like some quiet time myself", she said. Searching Jennie's face for clues, Perry agreed that the boys could ride with him. "Are you feeling well, Jennie? You have been quiet this morning. We could stay at our next camp for a couple of nights. Maybe you need extra time to rest." Jennie's eyes flashed with annoyance. "I am fine, Perry. I would like to have some time to myself, that's all", her voice cracked as she answered him.

Gathering the Duncan boys to himself, Perry cautiously glimpsed back at Jennie as he helped the boys climb to his wagon. "Pa, doesn't Ma want us to ride with her anymore? Jesse asked tearfully. "Naw, she just wants some time to herself to make plans for when we get to Sheridan. She likes to plan ahead and this will give her time to do that. Women folk like to have quiet time more than us men", he said.

The sun was rising over the horizon as the wagons pulled away from camp. Clouds in the expansive sky reflected deep red and purple streaks from east to west. Behind Jennie's wagon, Perry watched Jennie's wagon sway back and forth against the swirling colored sky. He thought to himself,

"What has changed Jennie's mood today? Something is going on."

As the wagons progressed northward, the prairie terrain changed from sandy white soil and monotonous flat sagebrush trail. Hills were steeper, stunted evergreen trees dotted the landscape and towering sandstone outcroppings created bizarre profiles along the trail. Off in the northwest distance, a silhouette of the Big Horn Mountains appeared. "Perry halted his wagon and called out loudly, "Jennie, those are the Big Horn Mountains!" Jennie stopped her wagon and looked around to see Perry. Jumping off the wagon, he ran to the side of her rig. "I see the mountains, Perry. We are still a long way from them " she said drearily.

CHAPTER 34

GLIMPSING THE BIG HORN MOUNTAINS

With the sight of the Big Horn Mountains growing more clearly, the Duncan boys grew more animated in their father's wagon. Wrestling and rolling around in the wagon was new behavior for the Duncan boys. Perry caught their enthusiasm. "We'll be going fishing in those mountains soon" he shouted into the back of the wagon.

Jennie's wagon ahead came to an abrupt halt. Jumping off the wagon, holding her mouth, Jennie ran to the front of the horses to be out of sight. Alarmed, Perry told the boys to stay in the wagon and ran to check on Jennie. He found her slumped over wiping vomit from her mouth. "Jennie, My God. What is happening?" "I'm just not feeling well, Perry. I may have eaten something that didn't agree with me. There isn't anything for you to worry about, really". Taking Jennie's arms, Perry lifted her to her feet. He could see that Jennie was tearful. "Jennie, we can stop and camp here for the night so you can get some rest. Do we have something in the larder for you to take?" She responded, "Perry, I feel better now.

Something was bothering my stomach and it is gone now. Go back to your wagon and let's get back on the trail."

As he walked away, he looked back at Jennie as she climbed back on her rig. Something about her demeanor was different. Perry's mood dampened as he steered his wagon behind Jennie's. Hours passed. It was unusually quiet behind him now. Perry glanced to the back of the wagon to see the Duncan boys had fallen asleep in the warmth of the day. Sprawled out like sleeping pups on their folded bedrolls, the youngsters' faces showed peacefulness. Jennie's wagon pushed forward up and down the hills of the trail without any sign of slowing. Finally, Perry whistled for Jennie to cease. She halted and looked around the side of the wagon to Perry.

Calling out to her, Perry said "We have to give the horses a break, Jennie. We have been on the trail for a long time now." Jennie pointed to the north and yelled back to Perry, "Just ahead is a stand of trees. It will be shady and we can take a break there." Without waiting for a response, Jennie lurched her wagon forward. Perry followed behind.

Jennie pulled her wagon under the shade of a leafy tree. She dismounted carrying a bucket before Perry arrived behind her. Before Perry reached her she was heading into the willows.

Perry followed Jennie into the thick willows. "Jennie, stop!" he called out to her. "Slow down, woman. Why the rush? When Jennie turned toward Perry, he saw that her face was flushed bright red and the hair around her face was wet with perspiration. "Jennie, Jennie, please stop. Let me help you" he pleaded.

Just as Perry caught up with Jennie, her knees buckled beneath her. She sank to the ground and cried out "We have to get to Sheridan, Perry." Kneeling at her side, Perry rested his hand on her shoulder. "We are making good time, Jennie. We are approaching the Powder River now. Once we get across the river, we'll find a camp site and settle in for the night. You are tired and you haven't eaten. You can't keep pushing hard like this. It isn't good for the horses either." There has to be some water here, Perry. I need to get water for the horses!" She cried out to him. "Did you hear what I just said, Jennie? We will get across the river and take care of the horses. They will drink plenty of water at the river." She looked up at Perry now standing above her. He gave her his hand and pulled her to her feet. Resting his hand on her forehead, he said "Jennie, you are burning up with fever. We'll be across the river in less than thirty minutes. Let's get these wagons to the other side and we'll quit for the night." Wobbly kneed, Jennie grasped Perry's hand as they wound their way back through the willows to the wagons. When they emerged from the brush, the Duncan boys stood waiting for their parents. Jesse ran to his mother and took her other hand. "Ma, do you need me to ride with you? I can drive the wagon, Ma. Let me help you." He said softly.

Jennie smiled at Jesse and tousled his hair. "You come with me Jesse. We'll get the wagon across the river." She said weakly. Perry lifted Jennie onto the wagon. Jesse followed, crawled over Jennie and sat tall next to her on the seat. Perry winked at Jesse and gave him a wave. "Take care of your Ma, son", he said.

CHAPTER 35

CROSSING THE POWDER RIVER

The Powder River flowed wide and gentle. Curving twice in less than three wagon lengths, it was more mud than water. As the horses reached the water, they stopped midstream to drink. "Don't let the horses stop, Jennie! Perry yelled loudly. Jennie jerked the reins up wildly to start them up. The horses heaved hard to get the wagon moving but the wheels had sunk into the mud up to the hub. Perry rushed his team to the other side of the river and jumped down. Running back to Jennie's wagon, Perry's arms waved in the air as he tried to run through the muddy water. When he reached Jennie's horses, he tugged the harness attempting to assist the team. The wheels continued to sink deeper into the dense mud. Perry called out to Jennie "Stay on the wagon, Jennie", then turned and ran back to his wagon on the other side. Frantically, he unhitched his horses and led them back into the river. He hitched them to the wagon beside Jennie's team and urged them forward. The wagon creaked and groaned as the wheels slowly moved forward through the thick heavy river bottom. Perry's face cringed in pain as he struggled to pull the horses forward.

On the other side of the river, Vere and Ike waved their arms and screamed out to their parents from the river bank. Their screams were not discernable to Perry and Jennie. Seemingly from nowhere, a horse with an Indian rider galloped into the water next to Jennie's stranded wagon. In horror, Perry's eyes widened as he looked up to see the Indian man at his side. He let go of the harness and fell backwards into the river. At that moment, Jennie too saw the young Indian man. He rode a horse with red feathers woven into the mane. The young man jumped from his horse into the river. Perry jumped to his feet and stood unmoving. "Let him help you, Perry !" Jennie shrieked. The young man got behind Jennie's wagon and pushed until the wheels were free of the burdensome river mud. Jennie managed to get the horses and wagon to solid ground near the river bank. Perry stood in the muddy water looking at the young Indian. He reached out his hand to the young man who returned his hand shake. Spellbound by the events that had taken place, the Duncan boys stood wide-eyed looking from one parent to the other in curiosity. Speechless, Jennie looked back to the young man. He held up his hand in a motionless wave. Jennie motioned for the man to come forward toward her. His eyes met hers then he returned to his horse and rode back across the river.

Walking backwards through the river, Perry watched the horse and rider splash swiftly through the water and disappear into the river willows on the bank. "What in God's name was that all about, Jennie?" Staring across the river, she said to Perry, "That is the rest of the story I have to tell you, Perry. I saw his horse tied up in Casper. I wasn't sure if it was his horse," she said in a daze. "Jennie, is he following us?" Perry questioned loudly. "I don't know, Perry. He is a good young man. He doesn't mean us any harm."

Cautiously watching the other side of the river, Perry began untying the extra team of horses from Jennie's wagon. "I have never had an experience like this, Jennie. Why did he rush to help us? How did he know we were here? Are there more Indians following us? Should we be arming ourselves"?

Leaning against the wagon, Jennie's face was red as fire. Her words slurred as she swayed trying to maintain her balance. "Perry, I need to rest a bit. Maybe Jesse can help you with the horses", she murmured. As she grasped the side board of the wagon, her hands slid down the side board to the ground. Perry rushed to her once again. "Jesse, take the horses and tie them up behind my wagon" Perry ordered. He called out to Vere "Get some cold water for your Ma. Wet a handkerchief from the side board and bring it to me". Perry cradled Jennie's head and slowly lowered her to the ground. "There is just too much excitement Jennie. Rest here a bit. You'll feel better with some cool water." Vere ran up from the river holding the dripping rag. He handed it to Perry, and then backed away. Perry gently patted Jennie's forehead and cheeks with the cool water. Her eyes closed as the water cooled her burning cheeks. Crouched on his knees next to Jennie, Perry spoke softly in her ear. "Rest my Jennie. We'll take care of everything. Just rest".

Perry motioned to Jesse to come to him. "Jesse, I need you to gather willow leaves from the trees at the bank. Do not go in the water, just gather the leaves off the branches and bring them to me. Take your brothers with you. You should all gather the leaves for me. Get a gunny sack from the wagon and fill it. Hurry now", he said urgently.

Jesse quickly got a sack and gathered his brothers. They ran to the river bank and shredded the leaves from the branches. When the sack was full, they ran to their Pa with the willow leaves.

Perry took a handful of the leaves, picked up a rock and crushed them in his hand. The green juice of the leaves formed tiny droplets and gathered in his cupped hand. He dipped his finger in the fluid and coated Jennie's parched lips with the fluid. As Jennie licked her lips, she cringed at the taste. "Jennie, this will make you feel better. You need to take more." Perry knelt by Jennie's side and continued to crush the leaves and coat Jennie's lips. As the summer sun slipped behind a western hill, Jennie's fever subsided. Her fiery cheeks calmed to pink. Silently sitting side by side, the Duncan boys watched their Pa tenderly care for their mother.

Perry looked up from Jennie's side to see his sons quietly following his every move. "Is Ma going to be okay, Pa" Jesse said. "She's going to be fine. We need to get some soup made for her. She needs to get some food in her after the long day." Opening her eyes, Jennie tried to sit up. Perry braced her back and lifted her up to a sitting position. "Well, young lady. It's about time you decide to join the world again. You pushed too hard today." She looked at Perry and said "What was that concoction you gave me?" He grinned and said "Willow leaf juice, Jennie. My Ma used to give it to us when we took down with a fever. I took a chance it would work for you too. We used to give it to the horses when their feet swelled up too." Rolling her eyes, she smiled at her husband. " I thought you were giving me whiskey. Your Ma was a wise woman".

Jennie rose to her feet with Perry's help. Holding on to his mother's skirt, Jesse escorted his Ma to the wagon. "Let's get Ma something to eat", Perry chirped. "Please no more willow leaves," Jennie teased.

Lifting Jennie in his arms, Perry gently placed Jennie on the seat of his wagon. "Jennie, I want you to go inside the wagon and lie down for a spell. I have to hitch up the horses and move the wagon up away from the river bank. If the river comes up during the night, we'll be right back in the mud again and God knows that young Indian won't be here to save us again. Is he some kind of an angel that just shows up when you need him?" Perry asked whimsically.

Jennie rested her head on the soft feather bedroll inside the wagon. She listened to Perry hitching up the horses and talking to the Duncan boys about what needed to be done. "Gather some firewood so we can get some soup started for your Ma. Don't go into the river. This is not a river for us to swim in. It is too muddy and murky. We'll swim at the next campsite." She listened as the Duncan boys scattered to gather fire wood. The wagon cover above Jennie's head swung back and forth as Perry moved the wagon off the river bank. Jennie realized that she had not laid on the floor of moving wagons since she was a child traveling with her parents to Colorado. The rocking sensation was reminiscent of those times. Closing her eyes, she remembered that innocent time when no worries beset her. When the wagon stopped, from the seat of the wagon, Perry pulled the curtain aside and looked in at Jennie. "How's my beautiful girl feeling now" he crooned to Jennie.

Bracing herself on her elbow, Jennie raised up and snapped "Perry Duncan, I am fine now. I can make dinner, you know. You just want to feed me more of that horse medicine, don't you?" " Some more of that medicine might help with that swelled head of yours, Jennie", he responded with a grin.

Lying her head back down in the wagon, Jennie drifted into a light sleep. The smell of cedar campfire smoke, the sound of clanking of pots and rustling of gunny sacks brought her back to consciousness. She rose to her knees and peeked through the wagon curtain to see Perry and the Duncan boys preparing soup. The fragrance of beef broth drifted her way in the summer evening air. A sudden burst of dizziness and nausea prompted Jennie to return to her prone position and wait for the sensation to pass.

Alone in the wagon, pondering her physical symptoms, Jennie reluctantly made a self- diagnosis. Once again she was with child. She recalled that these symptoms when she was pregnant with baby Lizzy. Her heart leapt in her chest as she reflected holding the tiny baby girl in her arms. She gently placed her hands over her stomach. Her cheeks blushed hot as the realization sunk deep into her heart. Baby Lizzy would be replaced, finally.

The wagon jerked to one side as Perry stepped up to bring a wooden bowl of soup to Jennie. He set the bowl on the seat and pulled the curtain aside. "Are you awake, Jennie? "he whispered. "Of course, I'm awake Perry. I am feeling much better now. I am able to join the rest of you outside to have soup. I don't like eating inside the wagon by myself on a beautiful evening like this. Please take the soup back down and I will join you there." Perry called Jesse and asked him to hold the soup while he helped Jennie leave the wagon. When Jennie's feet touched the ground, her legs shook. She quickly gained sure footing and pulled her arm away from Perry's grip. "I am good now, Perry", she announced.

Jennie felt like she was the main attraction as she sat around the campfire with her family. Each time she looked up from her bowl of soup, her children and Perry were staring intensely at her. "Please stop watching me", she called out, looking around at her family. "I had a spell of heat exhaustion but I am over it now and I feel fine." There is nothing to worry about!" Her response to the family had the desired effect on everyone. Perry engaged the boys in nonsensical conversation.

After the dinner, the Duncan boys rose from their seats and dutifully carried their bowls to the river. Perry reached for Jennie's empty bowl and followed his sons. Watching them file in line to the river, Jennie smiled. She wanted to announce to her family her suspicion about being pregnant, but decided to put the news to Perry's ears first. Closing her eyes, she wrapped her arms around her stomach and rocked on her seat. A baby girl would be born in Sheridan, Wyoming. Jennie's urgency to get to Sheridan was upon her family now. There could be no unexpected delays. The trip must commence early tomorrow morning.

CHAPTER 36
A NEW BABY

Jennie retired to the wagon to prepare for Perry's arrival. While waiting for Perry to come to bed, Jennie reached into the wagon box and pulled out her secretly wrapped pink flowered fabric. Holding the folded fabric to her chest, she closed her eyes and envisioned a tiny flowered dress for her newborn.

Perry bounded onto the wagon with force, rattling the contents of every compartment. Quickly hiding her secret package, Jennie sat with her legs folded under her on the soft bedroll. Stripping down to his underwear, Perry sprawled out beside Jennie. He pulled her down to his side and wrapped his arms around her waist as she lay on her side facing away from him. "We need a good night's sleep, Jennie. Just rest and I will keep an ear out for the boys. We all need to sleep so we can get an early start tomorrow." Whispering Perry's name, Jennie closed her eyes. "I have something to tell you", she said. Perry pushed her shoulder around to face her. "What, Jennie? Are you feeling ill again"?

"No Perry, I am not sick. I think we are going to have another baby."

Perry jumped to his knees, straddling Jennie as she lay. "Jennie, oh my Jennie! I should have known that is why you were feeling ill. We are having a baby in Wyoming!" Jennie nodded as she looked up into Perry's stunned face. He leaned down and kissed her forehead, her nose, her cheeks and her lips. "This is our new start, Jennie! We'll continue our new life in Sheridan with a new baby in the family." "I'll have to make a new cradle since we left the old one in Cherry Creek. I am so happy, Jennie. So happy", he repeated quietly.

Lying down next to Jennie, Perry took her hand in his and kissed it softly. "Get some sleep, Jennie," he whispered.

For two days, the Duncans' wagons trailed north and finally reached the foothills of the Big Horn Mountains. On the second night, they camped along a small creek known as Crazy Woman Creek. Augustine had told the story to Perry that the creek was named after a woman who was abandoned after the group she was traveling with was killed by a band of Indians, leaving her to wander in a canyon alone. Her screams were legend in the canyon where the creek originated. He said the canyon and creek bared the same name and that Perry should avoid the canyon area. Perry didn't tell his family the name of the creek or the reason for its name. On the third night, the Duncan family spent the night along Clear Creek just west of the small outpost of Buffalo, Wyoming. Fort Fetterman was situated just west of Buffalo. Clear Creek flowed fresh cold water from the Big Horn Mountains south of the fort. The Duncan boys waded and fished the creek, playing among the large smooth white rocks in the creek. Buffalo, the county seat of Johnson County, was a bustling small community of ranchers who raised cattle and sheep. The Main Street in town was built around Clear Creek. There were banks, saloons and a large Mercantile where the Duncans picked up a few supplies for the remainder of their trip. Perry was taken by the proximity of the mountains to the small community of Buffalo. He asked Jennie if she would like to make Buffalo her home. She answered Perry abruptly, "I am going to Sheridan, Wyoming, Perry". "But Jennie, we could homestead at the foot of these mountains. Hunting and fishing here is perfect for our family", he pleaded. Jennie answered again, "I am going to Sheridan, Wyoming, Perry Duncan. Are you going to join me?"

CHAPTER 37

FOLLOWING THE BOZEMAN TRAIL

Sheridan was a mere 30 miles north of Buffalo. The Duncan's followed the Bozeman Trail on their trek to Sheridan. Between Buffalo and Sheridan they encountered another fort called Fort Kearney. There had been several skirmishes involving the troops and native Indians at the fort. Perry pushed his family hard and fast to get beyond the area in hopes of avoiding confrontations with Indians. After leaving Buffalo, the family camped along Piney Creek just south of Sheridan. Uniformed men stopped by the Duncan campsite and advised the Duncan's that they were in territorial lands and to be watchful at their campsite. Jennie spent time walking the fields near the campsite and told Perry that she wanted to be living near this area. Perry resisted. "Jennie, we are in a dangerous area here. Let's go north a bit further, closer to Sheridan and find some flat farm ground where we can homestead". Reluctantly, Jennie agreed.

When morning broke over the eastern sky, the Duncans were loaded and ready to push to Sheridan. Filled with anticipation, they followed the ruts of the Bozeman Trail and drove the wagons till deep into the evening. About ten miles south of Sheridan, they stopped for the night among lush green hillsides and tall cottonwood trees. Wild plum and chokecherry trees in the tiny valleys were heavy with summer fruit. Jennie announced to the family, "This is our new home. In the morning, we will unhitch the wagons and I will take a horse into town to stake our claim for this land. Perry, you will stay here with the boys and I will take care of the homesteading forms. Someone must stay with the land and our belongings while I make the necessary arrangements."

Perry awoke to sounds outside the wagon. It was barely light outside. He reached over to touch Jennie, only to find that she was not beside him. Crawling to the curtain, he looked outside and saw Jennie's barely visible form against the early dawn light. "Jennie," he called out. "What are you doing up so early?" She called back, "I am going to Sheridan, Perry. I told you last night I would be leaving early." "But Jennie, you haven't eaten. In your condition, you need to eat to keep the baby healthy." Noticeably annoyed, Jennie responded, "Perry Duncan, I know what I have to do. You take care of the boys while I am gone. I'll be back as soon as I am finished with the homesteading paperwork. You can start scouting out a new home site when it gets light. We need to find a natural water source near our home site. This is where we will live." Jennie lifted herself onto a horse and rode off as Perry squinted in the darkness to watch her leave.

After she disappeared into the darkness, Perry fell back onto his buttocks. He brushed the hair from his face and sat in the dark wagon. Looking around the wagon stillness, he fell backwards onto the bedroll. "I'm home," he thought. To himself, he whispered "This is where I live until the day I die".

In the peace of the early morning, Perry drifted off to sleep again.

"Pa! Wake up Pa!" Jesse called from outside. Confused and dazed, Perry sat up and looked around. He wasn't sure if it was day or night. Slowly he regained his senses, remembering Jennie leaving on a horse in the wee hours of the morning. "What, son? I'm awake. I'll be outside in a minute" he responded. Sleepy-eyed, he grabbed his clothes and hurried from the wagon.

"Pa, one of our horses is missing!" Jessie yelled. Relaxing his tense shoulders, Perry told Jesse that his Ma took the horse to Sheridan in the early morning. "We are going to scout out a place to build our home, son." Get your brothers up and we'll make some breakfast before we find a good place. Ma wants us to find a place with good water and trees. "

Jesse turned and loped back to the wagon. After raucous commotion in the boy's wagon, the Duncan boys joined their father outside.

With his hands on his hips, Perry addressed his sons. "Sons, we have work to do this morning. Your Ma has gone into Sheridan to complete the paperwork to make this our new home. We'll have some fruit and cheese this morning for breakfast and then we'll set out to find a place to build our home. Your Ma is counting on us to find the perfect spot. Can we do that?" Anxiously, they nodded to their father.

Perry packed his pistol under his belt and a canteen of water hung from the belt loop of his britches. Each of the boys carried a walking stick brought with them from Cherry Creek. Leading the way, Perry walked through the tall grass, looking toward a hill to the west of where the wagons veered off the Bozeman Trail wheel ruts. "Watch out for snakes, sons", he called back. "Use your sticks to move the tall grass aside in front of you". The Duncan boys' heads barely reached the tops of the native grass.

When they reached the summit of an east sloping hill, a spacious lush valley with a small pond spread before them to the west. High above the horizon, the tall snowcapped peaks of the Big Horn Mountains stood majestic against the deep blue sky. Perry viewed the expanse of valley and pointed to a spot near the pond. "There it is. That's the place", he spoke smiling. The valley was rich with deep green grass. Wild fruit trees were abundantly tucked into narrow gullies winding their way to the pond. Situated with protection from the northwest winds, Perry was certain that his eyes beheld the Duncan family's new home site. Concealed in tall foliage, mule deer scattered in the meadows as the group began their descent into the valley. Holding their walking sticks above their heads, the Duncan boys jogged down the hillside to the bottom of the draw. As they reached the edge of the pond, they squealed in delight as woodland ducks took flight over their heads from the water. Behind them, Perry took in the grandeur of the wide landscape of untouched beauty of this newfound Wyoming paradise. "I can't wait for Jennie to see this", he whispered to himself. "You were right, Jennie. This is our new home".

Perry and the Duncan boys spent a good part of the morning exploring their valley. Wildlife of every species occupied the trees, the shrubs, the pond and the sky above. While traversing the bottom land, they came upon a mound of dirt with a large hole in the ground below. Perry cautioned the boys to stand back from the hole. As they backed away, a large badger stuck his head up from the hole. Without provocation, the animal rapidly charged in the direction of the Duncan brothers, growling furiously and showing its vicious teeth. Perry seized his pistol and shot the animal just before it reached the boys. Shaken by the experience, the boys grew wary of further exploration. "Let's go back to the wagon, Pa", Vere whimpered. "It's okay, sons. We know what to look for now. This was our first hunting trip on our place. You can name your first pony Badger to remember this day."

CHAPTER 38

THE LOGS ARRIVE

Afternoon sun had sunk to the west. Perry suggested they head back to the wagon to get ready for Jennie's return. "Wait till your Ma sees the place we found to build our house. It has everything she wants!" he said. The cheerful tone in his voice carried in the air as they climbed out of the valley toward the wagon. When they reached the top of the hill, the young Duncan's were breathless and rosy cheeked. Their tiny legs had carried them farther than they were accustomed.

While walking back to the wagon, Perry noticed a dust cloud rising above the hills to the north. It was coming from the direction Jennie took when she left early in the morning. As they arrived back at their wagon, they could hear loud creaking sounds coming from that direction. As the dust cloud grew closer, Jennie appeared on her horse over a hill. Behind her was a large flatbed wagon piled high with roughhewn pine logs driven by two men.

Jennie trotted her horse to the waiting Duncan's. Before dismounting, she called to Perry, "Where should we unload the logs, Perry?" Perry walked to Jennie's side. "Jennie, what have you done?" We are a long way from the home site we chose!" Waving her arms, she signaled the drivers of the flatbed wagon to halt.

"Perry Duncan, we have hauled these logs for ten miles. Show me where you want the logs to be unloaded. Jump on this horse with me and we'll guide these men to the location." "But what about the boys, Jennie? Can we leave them here by themselves?" Jennie blurted back "They will be fine, Perry. We are in a safe area. You can help the men unload the wood and I'll return to the boys as soon as I see the area you chose for the house."

Perry looked down at the Duncan boys as they stood listening to Jennie's orders. "Jesse, you need to stay here with your brothers while we are gone. You are in charge of taking care of them. Just stay by the wagons and don't run off somewhere. Your Ma will be back soon. I'm counting on you to be strong and keep your brothers safe". Jesse put his shoulders back and nodded to his father, "I will Pa. I'll take care of Vere and Ike. I'll be strong like you, Pa."

Winking at his sons, he jumped on the horse with Jennie. Jesse, Vere and Ike watched their parents ride off to the west with the hefty creaking wagon following behind.

After the long trek from Sheridan, Jennie's horse resisted her insistence that he haste up the hill to the west. The wagon with the logs lagged behind, sluggishly climbing to the summit behind Perry and Jennie's horse. Once on top of the hill, Perry jumped off the horse, spread his arms wide overlooking the valley and pointed out to Jennie's his choice of a home site. "Perry, it is a perfect location for our new home!" she said. She leapt from her horse, threw her arms around Perry's neck and squeezed him firmly. Perry spoke softly in her ear, "Jennie, you were right to bring us here to Wyoming. We have a new start here with our sons and our new baby on the way. I'll make sure of that. Now, tell me one thing. "How did you arrange for a wagon full of logs to follow you back here?" "It was easy, Perry, I simply went to the lumber mill and told them I was building a home and needed enough wood to do the job. I also have 18 boxes of nails on that wagon and a red banner to mark our new home location. We need to start the house soon so we can be under a roof before cold weather sets in."

The log wagon finally reached the top of the hill and Perry pointed out the location where it was to be unloaded. He told Jennie to return to the boys as he jumped on the side of the lumber wagon. "I'll catch a ride back with this wagon when we finish unloading the logs," he called back to Jennie. Turning her horse, she loped down the hill toward the Duncan boys.

While the wagon screeched gradually down the steep hill toward the prospective home site, Perry hung on to the steel side brace, leaning out like a rider on a San Francisco trolley car taking in the sights. A cool breeze ruffled his long hair as the wagon descended. Full of anticipation, Perry closed his eyes and breathed in the fragrant summer air.

At the bottom of the hill, Perry jumped off the wagon and led the way to a flat area near the pond where the lumber would be stacked. The wagon drivers left their positions on the seat and walked to Perry. After a brief introduction and conversation, one of the drivers unhitched his team and led the horses to the pond for water. Perry walked through the tall grass picking up rocks, clearing the way for the logs.

"Okay, Mr. Duncan, let's get started unloading this wood", one of the men shouted. He reached into the wagon box and threw a pair of leather gloves to Perry. "Thank you kindly", Perry replied.

"I wasn't prepared for hard labor this afternoon but I sure appreciate your help", he bellowed with a full smile.

The three men worked an assembly line of unloading the logs. Perry held the last place in the line, stacking the logs in a pile. As he placed the last log on the stack, it began to collapse. He reached into the stack and tried to stop the movement of the stack, but the logs continued to roll down on top of him. His arms were trapped under several heavy logs. Still unable to move his arms, the stack rumbled down, crushing his arms and chest. Trembling, Perry remembered his father's death from being crushed by railroad ties in Colorado.

Rushing to help Perry, the two men from the wagon were able to free Perry's arms from the log pile. Screaming in pain, Perry sunk to the ground. One arm was clearly broken with the bone protruding from the skin, bleeding profusely. Whipping the scarf from his neck, one of the men applied a tourniquet above Perry's elbow. They quickly loaded Perry onto the wagon, one of the men remaining beside him on the flatbed as they rushed toward the hill to get him back to his family. With every bump the wagon crossed over, Perry grimaced in pain, in spite of the man's attempts to brace his arm from moving when the wagon swayed and lurched. The driver of the wagon made every attempt to find smooth ground to travel and frequently looked back to Perry and his partner. "Mr. Duncan, I am going as fast as I can. I am sorry about the rough ride", he yelled back.

The sleeve of Perry's shirt was blood soaked red. Before the log wagon reached Jennie, the Duncan boys had run out to meet it and saw their Pa lying on the flatbed. Running beside the wagon as it progressed toward Jennie; Jesse called out, "Ma, Pa is hurt. Pa needs help Ma!" Hurrying to the wagon, Jennie held her hands over her mouth as she saw Perry lying on the flatbed. The wagon came to a halt and Jennie jumped up to be at Perry's side. Pale faced, Perry said "Jennie, I'll be fine. Get me to the wagon and we'll get this stitched up. You've stitched up horses and cattle. Get my whiskey from the wagon box. Boys, go and find some willow leaves for me." The wagon drivers stood nearby helplessly. Jennie approached them and said "I need your help to get that arm bone put back."

The older of the drivers said, "Mam, we'll do what we can but maybe Mr. Duncan should be taken into Sheridan to see a doctor.' Jennie clutched the man's arm and pulled him aside. She hissed with her teeth clenched "We are going to take care of this right now. I need one of you to hold him down while one of you puts that bone back in where it belongs. I'm getting the whiskey for him right now and get some of that into him and onto his wound. This will take a bit of time. Please stay here with me to get this done", she said sternly. The two drivers looked at each other in disbelief. The older man said, "I'll hold Mr. Duncan down". Jennie rushed to the wagon and came back with Perry's whiskey bottle. She knelt down next to him and put the bottle to his mouth. "Perry, drink this. I want you to take several large gulps. Do, it Perry", she urged him. Perry complied with Jennie's orders. His body shivered as he gulped down the potent whiskey. "Keep drinking, Perry", she said as she poured the whiskey down his throat. Perry closed his eyes after drinking the whiskey. Jennie retrieved her sewing basket from the wagon. She got a large leather work needle and a spool of heavy silk thread from the box. Lighting a match, she heated the needle and laid it aside. Perry looked up at Jennie through half open eyes. Slurring his words, he said, "Let's get this done." The younger wagon driver looked at Jennie in distress and said, "Mam, I don't know what I am supposed to do with this arm." Jennie firmly replied, "Here's what you have to do. You must take the arm and push the end of the bone that is sticking up through the skin back down to meet up with the other part of the bone. We will hold Mr. Duncan down while you do this but you need to do it in one quick motion. No matter how Mr. Duncan screams, you need to get this done so I can get this arm stitched up." Bleary-eyed, Perry looked up and yelled, "Do what she says, man!" Jennie replied to the young man, "When I give you the signal, do it."

Jennie stooped over Perry and brushed the damp curls off his forehead. "Okay, Perry, we are going to fix this arm." Perry opened his eyes just as Jennie motioned to the young man to put the arm bone back. With a loud snap the bone was pushed down. Perry wailed loudly. Jennie poured the whiskey over the broken skin on Perry's arm as he writhed on the floor of the flatbed, groaning fitfully. Straightening up from her stooped position, Jennie saw the small Duncan boys standing at the foot of the wagon holding their bags of willow leaves. The children's faces were scrunched in terror as they watched their Pa rolling on the rough floor of the wagon in extreme pain. "Get me a clean handkerchief from the wagon, Jesse", she called out. Dropping his bag of leaves, Jesse ran to the wagon. He returned clutching a white handkerchief in his trembling hands. Jennie took the rag and soaked it with whiskey. "Perry, you need to hold still while I stitch this cut on your arm. I know this will hurt but I will make it fast", she whispered. Her hand was sure and steady as she pulled the skin together and stitched the wound closed. Perry clamped his teeth and stared into the blue sky. When she finished stitching the wound, she wrapped the whiskey soaked rag around Perry's arm and held it tightly for a few minutes. Perry's face, drenched in cold sweat, was pale and drawn. Jennie blotted his face and neck with a cool wet rag while the wagon drivers watched in anguish. "Mam, we have to get this wagon back to Sheridan before dark. Are you sure we shouldn't take Mr. Duncan with us?" the older gentleman asked. Before Jennie could answer, Perry blurted out "I'm not going anywhere. Just help me off this flatbed." Perry slowly sat up and swung his legs over the side of the wagon. With Jennie at his side, the two men assisted Perry to his feet. Holding him under his armpits, they helped him to the wagon back board. Breathlessly, Perry asked, "Where are those willow leaves, boys? Jennie, girl, make me up some of that horse medicine". Rushing to their Pa, the Duncan boys brought their bags of leaves. Jennie pulled out a handful of leaves. "These are not willow leaves. Where did you find these? Perry, we will be back in a bit. Come with me sons, and we will find some willow branches for Pa", she said in exasperation.

The wagon drivers stepped forward and told Jennie they would be leaving. "We can take Mr. Duncan to town and have him back here tomorrow", the younger man reiterated. Jennie thoughtfully looked back to Perry. "Thank you, gentlemen, I think he will be fine. If Mr. Duncan needs further help, I will take him into town myself". Glancing back at Perry, they reluctantly boarded their wagon and left the Duncan's campsite.

Before leaving Perry in search of willow leaves, Jennie instruct-ed Jesse to stay with his Pa. "Vere, Ike and I will find the leaves, Jesse. You stay here with your Pa and make sure he doesn't try to get up and walk around." She went to Perry as he slumped against the side of the wagon. "Perry, I am going to help you to lie down till we get back. Lie down on your good side until we return." She gently braced his body as he lay down on the backboard. "I'll take care of Pa", Jesse said proudly.

Holding the younger Duncan boys' hands, Jennie hurried to a stand of trees in a small gully just over the closest hill. Jennie found some small willows nestled amongst the tall clover. Pointing out the willow branches to the youngsters, they gathered leaves, filling their sacks. "Let's get back to Pa and Jesse. Now you know where the willow trees are if Pa needs more", she said. As they walked from the gully, Jennie showed the boys that the leaves they gathered earlier were from narrow leaf cottonwood trees. She showed them the differences in the leaves, noting that the cottonwood leaves were wider than the willows and slightly different shaped.

Perry was asleep when Jennie and her boys returned from gathering willow leaves. Sitting crossed legged on the ground under the back board, Jesse told his Ma that Perry had not moved. "I hope Pa isn't dead, Ma", he whimpered. "Your Pa is just sleeping off the whiskey, Jesse", she answered him sympathetically. "When he wakes up we need to get some of the willow juice into him to stop the swelling". Jennie went to her wagon and brought out a small glass jar and mortar and pestle she used to grind herbs from her garden in Cherry Creek. The Duncan boys watched as she ground the willow leaves to a green paste. Carefully, she drained the juice from the paste into the glass jar. Jennie continued until the leaves were used up as the jar filled with the pungent green willow juice.

As dusk moved in on the Duncan family, Perry stirred from his slumber. He moved sluggishly from the back board calling for Jennie. When Jennie heard him calling, she rushed to his side. He grasped her arm to pull himself up from the prone position. "Jennie, I need some more whiskey. I can't bear this pain." he mumbled. She reached into her pocket and pulled out the bottle of willow juice for Perry. "Have some of this horse medicine first, Perry", she smiled at him as she handed the jar to him. "Don't drink it all at once. We'll make some more but this is all we have now". Perry sipped the juice and handed the bottle back to Jennie. Reaching into her other pocket, Jennie brought out Perry's whiskey bottle. "Take it slow with this Perry. Tomorrow we will go into Sheridan so you can see the doctor there. He will surely have some opium we can bring home for you". From deep in her apron pocket she brought out a bottle of deep purple liquid called gentian violet. "I'm going to put some of this liquid on your wound, Perry. Jennie dabbed the deep purple concoction on Perry's wound and helped him from the back board into the wagon. Pondering how long it would take for Perry to be able to use the arm again, she touched his forehead and covered him with a wool blanket.

Preparing dinner for the children, Jennie daydreamed about her new home in Sheridan. Her plan was to begin constructing the log home immediately. Perry's accident would delay the plan now unless she could find someone to help her with the construction. She couldn't wait for Perry's arm to heal to get the work started.

Sending the Duncan boys into their bedrolls, Jennie told them to stay in the wagon. "We'll be taking your Pa into Sheridan early tomorrow morning. Nobody leaves this wagon tonight. Do you understand?" Together they responded, "Yes, Ma".

Jennie crept silently into the wagon next to Perry as he lay sleeping. Closing her eyes, she tried to sleep. Her mind ran in circles as she tried to envision what to do next since Perry was injured. She had to have the house construction finished by the time the new baby would arrive. They could not survive a Wyoming winter in a covered wagon. Jennie sat up. Reaching over to the side of the wagon, she took Perry's bottle of whiskey in her hand. Tilting the bottle back, she swallowed a large gulp. Her body quaked as the whiskey seared down her throat. Looking down at her sleeping husband in the dimming light, Jennie lay down beside him and waited for sleep to release her.

"Jennie, please, I need you to help me. I am hurting pretty badly", Perry whispered in the night. Bolting up from a sound sleep, Jennie felt around in the dark for the lantern. Still groggy, she toppled the lantern. Quickly up righting the lantern, she struck a match to light it. A small amount of kerosene that had dripped from the lantern erupted in flames on the feather bed. Frantically, Jennie let out a fearsome scream, beating at the flames with her night dress. Struggling to sit up, Perry got to his knees and helped Jennie put out the flames. Filled with acrid smoke from the smoldering feathers, the inside of the wagon, was gray with sooty residue. "Okay, Jennie. We're fine now. We need to go outside to get some fresh air." Jennie helped Perry get moved to the seat outside the wagon. She hooked the heavy curtain open and drug the thick feather bed outside, still smoking from the fire. After dousing the featherbed with water, Jennie knelt on the ground sobbing. "Perry, why is everything going wrong today? We finally made it here and I thought everything was going to work out. This is dreadful", she whimpered. "Jennie, the hardest part of the move is over. C'mon now, get me that whiskey bottle and some of that horse medicine. Tomorrow will be a better day. Actually, it is tomorrow now. Today will be a better day, Jennie. It feels like morning is just around the corner. How about we get started to Sheridan early"? Handing the whiskey bottle to Perry, Jennie touched his fingers as he grasped the bottle from her. "I'll get that horse medicine for you, Mister Duncan", she said softly.

Jennie heard the Duncan boys chattering inside their wagon. There was no light on the horizon yet. Carrying the lantern, she stood outside hoping to hear what the commotion was all about. Jesse peeked from the wagon curtain "Ma, can we come out now? You said we weren't allowed to leave the wagon. We heard you scream, Ma. Is Pa sick, Ma?" Jennie reassured Jesse, "Pa is doing okay now. We are going to leave early for Sheridan so you need to get yourselves dressed. Fold up your bedrolls before you come out", she ordered.

CHAPTER 39

BROKEN ARM

It wasn't daylight yet and Jennie's body felt weary. Her eyes were heavy from lack of sleep. She climbed back on the wagon and delivered the horse medicine to Perry. He quickly took two swigs of the green juice and leaned his head back on the canvas spine. "Jennie, I'll be fine in a bit. Once we get into Sheridan to the dispensary, I know there will be something they can do for me there and I won't be such a burden to you", he said. She lifted the lantern to light Perry's face. "Perry, you are not a burden to me. You are always the man with the right answers. I should have waited to get the logs for our house but I wanted us to get started right away. I'll take care of you and you'll be back to health in no time", she said cheerfully. Lifting herself onto the wagon seat next to Perry, she tenderly kissed his forehead. "Now, get into the back, Perry. We will be heading out shortly and I want you settled in with blankets bracing your arm as we travel into Sheridan. It is a rough ride in places. I'll have Jesse ride in back with you to keep you company", she said as she helped Perry lie down inside the wagon. "How about another shot of whiskey, Jennie?" Perry shouted to her as she gathered the boys into the wagon. "You can have one more for the ride in to Sheridan, Perry. After we get to Sheridan, we'll see what the doctor says about the whiskey".

Perry Duncan's Adams apple twitched as he took a long gulp of whiskey from the nearly empty bottle. He handed the bottle to Jesse who sat beside him in the wagon. "Put the cork back in, son", he said to Jesse. Jesse pushed the cork as hard as he could but couldn't get it lodged firmly into the mouth of the bottle. "Aw hell, son. Just give me the bottle and I'll finish it off", Perry slurred to Jesse. Handing his Pa the bottle, Jesse turned to see if his Ma was watching. When the bottle was empty, Perry handed it back to Jesse and laid his head down. Jennie looked back just as Perry closed his eyes. Jesse sat shamefaced with the empty whiskey bottle between his legs. "Jesse, I told you to watch your Pa and make sure his arm was cushioned for the ride. I didn't tell you to get him stone drunk for the trip", she said sternly. "But Ma, he said it wasn't much and he would finish it so it wouldn't spill. He wanted to go to sleep."

Creeping the wagon toward Sheridan in an attempt to make the trip less jarring on Perry's arm, Jennie regularly looked back to Perry and Jesse in the back of the wagon. Noticing that Perry's shirt was becoming wet with perspiration around the neck, she asked Jesse to try and wake up his Pa. Jesse gently wiggled Perry's good arm to revive him, with no response from his Pa. "Shake him harder, Jesse! Jennie called back. Stopping the wagon, Jennie dove into the back of the wagon and softly slapped Perry's cheeks to get a response from him. His eyes slowly opened. She felt his forehead, noting that it was wet with sweat and hot to the touch. "Perry, I'm going to give you more willow juice since you feel fever-ish", she said softly. Leaning up on his good elbow, Perry took in the juice and lay back down. Jumping back on her seat, Jennie pushed the wagon forward more quickly. She felt an urgency to get Perry to Sheridan in spite of the pain of a fast moving wagon ride. Vere and Ike were bouncing wildly on the seat next to her as she hurried over the rough terrain. "You boys get in the back with Jesse but don't get too close to your Pa", she ordered.

Jennie's wagon pulled into Sheridan on a dusty worn street not far from the lumber mill. Jumping off the wagon, she ran to the mill. "Where is the doctor in this town? She called out to two men standing near the back of the building. When the men turned around, she recognized them as the same men who delivered the logs. "Hello, Mrs. Duncan", one of the men responded. "The dispensary is down the road in the log building next to the train station", he said. "Is your husband not doing well?" She responded, "Mr. Duncan needs to see a doctor as soon as possible." One of the men jumped on the seat next to Jennie as she boarded the wagon. "I'll help you get Mr. Duncan off the wagon", he said.

Perry could scarcely talk as they arrived at the dispensary. Jennie and her accomplice struggled to get him out of the wagon. Sweat poured down Perry's face as he got his feet on the ground. Jennie and the lumber man braced Perry with each taking a side grip on Perry's leather belt. He yelled out in pain as he walked to the door of the dispensary. Once inside, a bald headed man wearing a white apron and thick glasses helped to get Perry to a cot in a spacious whitewashed room with shelves of bottles. A wooden table covered with white cloth held metal instruments near the cot. My name is Doctor Shenk. "What do we have here"? He said as he assisted Perry to lie down on the cot. Mumbling incoherently, Perry kept his eyes closed. "Sir, what is your name?' he asked Perry. Perry didn't respond to Dr. Shenk's inquiry. The doctor looked to Jennie and asked. "What is this man's name and what has happened to him?" Apprehensively, Jennie told the doctor that his name was Perry Duncan. She added that she was his wife and that he broke his arm while stacking logs for their new home.

"How long has he been like this, Mrs. Duncan?" Jennie responded. "about 6 hours". Dr. Shenk proceeded to unwrap the dressing on Perry's arm. "Mrs. Duncan, your husband may have a serious infection in this arm. This is what we call a compound fracture where the bone protruded through the skin. This protrusion may have introduced bacteria into the arm." Jennie became defensive with the doctor, saying "I understand this Dr. Shenk. I did everything I could to keep the wound clean. What can you do for him?" "I will start giving him sulfur pills and wash the wound. There is nothing I can do to straighten the arm now. I will also give him opium for the pain until the infection clears up. You will have to leave him here with me for a day or so until I think he is showing signs of improvement. I have a separate room in the back where he can rest and I can watch him. I live in this building and my wife, Rose will assist me in his care." "Dr. Shenk, will my husband be well again?" Jennie's voice cracked as she asked the doctor. "He looks like a strong man, Mrs. Duncan. He has a better than average chance of getting better quickly but he needs to be watched here by me and my wife." Jennie walked to Perry's cot, stooped down and kissed his cheek. "I'll be close by, Perry. Listen to what the doctor tells you and we will get a boarding room somewhere close by. As soon as you are well, the boys and I will take you back to our wagon." Lifting his hand to touch Jennie's face, Perry opened his eyes and smiled weakly at his wife. Parched and pale, his lips stuck together as he tried to talk to her. "Okay, Jennie", he whispered.

Jennie walked to the door with the doctor. "I will stop in the morning, Dr. Shenk. Please take good care of this man", she said.

Just down the road next to the railroad tracks, Jennie parked her wagon and entered the Sheridan Inn. It was a large boarding house with a wooden dance floor and rooms above the intricately carved wooden bar and saloon. Loud piano music resonated in the room. Glancing around the room, Jennie noticed that every stool at the bar was occupied. She walked up to the desk and inquired about a room for the night. As she spoke to the attendant, the men sitting on the stools turned to watch her. Noticing the stares of the men, she said loudly, "My three children will be staying with me tonight."

"Bring your bedrolls with you to the room", Jennie instructed her sons. She gathered items from the wagon and packed them in to a large straw basket. Reaching under the seat, Jennie retrieved her burlap wrapped gun and placed it in the basket. Ascending the large wooden staircase, Jennie and her sons marched to their room above the saloon.

CHAPTER 40

BURNING AT THE INN

Late into the night the noise and tobacco smoke from the saloon drifted into the Duncan's room above. Raucous laughter was so loud it seemed that the revelers were dancing in the room with the Duncan boys and Jennie. Covering her head, Jennie tried to blot out the music and laughter. The Duncan boys drifted off to sleep in spite of the calamity. When silence finally came, Jennie slept. After a few hours of sound sleep, Jennie was awakened by the smell of smoke in her room. "This is not tobacco smoke", she thought. Rising from her bed, she rushed to the window and saw flames and black smoke shooting out of the window below her room. She could feel the heat on the floor beneath her feet. Scrambling to her sons' bed, she shook the children and yelled for them to wake up. "Run to the door! Get out of the room and run downstairs!" She shrieked. Grasping her straw basket, shoes and dress, she followed behind the children as they fled the room in their under clothes. She glanced back into the room just as flames from below penetrated the floor by the window. Running back into the room, Jennie swept up the pile of her sons' clothing and darted to the door again. Stopping abruptly, she turned around and flung the stack of the Duncan boys' cherished clothing into the flames. For a moment, she stood unmoving watching her sons' clothing envelop in the angry flames. Dense brown smoke curled above the hissing pile of flannel and oil cloth clothing. Dashing out the door, Jennie didn't stop until she was outside with her sons. Standing in the grassy area, they watched as flames spread to the roof of the building.

Shivering in the cool night air, the Duncan boys, clad in their sheer night shirts, gathered around their mother. In the distance the sound of a bell rang furiously. Approaching at a high rate of speed, a horse drawn water wagon arrived in a cloud of dust. Jennie pushed her sons from the path of the wagon as two men jumped off the wagon with large canvas hoses. A third man remained at the rear of the wagon rapidly pumping a handle to deliver water to the hoses. The fire, which had burned the Duncan's room and part of the saloon below, was soon extinguished. As the Duncan's stood absorbed, Jesse looked to his mother and sobbed, "Ma, our shoes and our new clothes are still in the room! We need our new clothes, Ma".

Jennie glared down and yelled, "Jesse, you stop this nonsense right now. We are lucky to have escaped with our lives and you are worried about clothes! I don't want to hear any more about your clothes. There are clothes in the wagon for you to wear." Jesse timidly responded, "Ma, our old clothes are back in the other wagon." Jennie smirked as she reached into the straw basket, pulled out her shawl and wrapped it around her shoulders. "We'll be fine," she said, patting little Ike on the head.

The street, crowded with ranting onlookers quickly filled with wagons carrying water troughs around the dim gas light pole. Jennie whispered "Let's get into the wagon, boys". One by one the barefooted children crossed the street and hoisted themselves into the wagon. Following behind, Jennie looked around the darkened empty wagon and realized that the boys' bedrolls were also left in the burning room. Reaching under the seat, Jennie pulled out an old horse blanket which she wrapped around the three children. "I'll find something for you to wear", she mumbled. Opening one of the wagon boxes, she slowly lifted a stack of Lizzy's dresses. Handing a dress to each of the boys, she snapped, "Put these clothes on until we get back to the other wagon". As Jesse unfolded the dress, he flung it across the wagon. "I'm not wearing this dress, Ma! Pa said we didn't have to wear these girl clothes ever again". Clutching Jesse's arm, Jennie jerked him around to look in his face. "Pick up the dress and put it on, JESSICA", she hissed. Crumpling in tears, Jesse picked up the dress and pulled it over his head. Watching in horror, Vere and Ike hurriedly pulled their dresses on as well. Sitting side by side on the wagon floor, the Duncan boys stared at their mother in quiet fear of her next outburst. "We'll wait here till daybreak, then go to the dispensary to see how your Pa is doing", she said. "Lie down, pull the blanket over you, and rest now. I don't want to hear any more complaints from any of you." The Duncan boys complied with their mother's orders.

Jennie reached into the straw basket and pulled out her dress. The dress reeked of smoke as she lifted it on over her night clothes. Leaning back against the sideboard, she took a deep breath and closed her eyes. Laying her hands over the slight bump on her stomach, she softly caressed it as if to comfort the child within her. Her heart thumped hard as she calmed herself. She knew that Perry would disapprove of his sons wearing Lizzy's clothes again, but she had no choice. Looking down at her children lying in Lizzy's clothes, Jennie whispered, "Jessica, Vera and Iris."

Loud clanking on the rail tracks woke Jennie from her early morning sleep. She peeked through the curtain to see wisps of smoke still rising like thin white funnels from the Sheridan Inn roof. The crowd continued to gather around the building. Jennie pulled her tousled hair back tightly and braided it. Glancing at her children still sleeping, she crept from the back of the wagon. Jumping off the wagon, she checked the horses and quietly carried a bucket of feed to them from the rear wagon box. After the horses were fed, she climbed back up on the seat, took the reins in hand and pushed the team forward. As she pulled up in front of the Sheridan Dispensary, Jesse called to her from inside the wagon. Jennie separated the curtain to look inside. Facing her, the boys looked down as she spoke to them. "Let's go in and see how your Pa is doing", she said. Jesse blurted out "No, Ma. We aren't going in there. We don't want Pa to see us dressed like this!" Saying nothing, Jennie abruptly yanked the curtain closed and left the wagon.

Once inside the dispensary, Jennie looked around the empty room for Perry. Dr. Shenk entered the room from the back. "Mr. Duncan is doing much better today, Mrs. Duncan", he said. "I believe you can take him home with you today." Jennie stood motionless. She said, "We'll do that, Dr. Shenk. The trouble is, we have no home to take him to yet." At that moment, Perry appeared in the doorway with his arm bandaged in a sling. Leaning on the door jamb, pale, but clean shaven, he grinned widely when he saw Jennie. "I am ready to leave with my family, Dr. Shenk. Thank you kindly for patching me up and helping me get through the night." Handing a brown glass bottle of medicine to Jennie, Dr. Shenk said, "Mr. Duncan will need to take a swig on this every few hours till the pain gets better. You'll need to keep the wound clean and he can't use the arm for a while but he'll do fine. Bring him back in to see me in two weeks."

Searching the room, Perry asked, "Where are the boys, Jennie?" Jennie responded sternly, "They chose to stay in the wagon, Perry.

"It's a long story Perry. A lot happened last night. There was a fire at the Sheridan Inn and all the clothes were burned. The only clothes I had for them were some of Lizzy's clothes. They had to put something on since we left the building in our night clothes as it was burning. They are very upset about not having their new clothes to wear."

"Jennie, I heard the fire bells ringing during the night! Are you all okay?" "We are fine, Perry. We got out of the room just before the flames overtook it. The boys clothing, shoes and bedrolls are gone. We'll have to stop at the Mercantile to get some supplies before we head back to the other wagon. We don't have the money to buy new clothes but we have to get them shoes and bedrolls", she announced. Perry's face contorted in worry. "Jennie, we have to find them something besides Lizzy's clothes to wear. We just can't make them wear those damned dresses." Jennie's eyes flashed in anger at Perry. "They will wear the clothes you cut up for them Perry! We can't be buying them new clothes right now!"

Standing nearby, Dr. Shenk overheard the discussion between the Duncan's.

"Mr. and Mrs. Duncan, I couldn't help but to overhear about the children's clothing being lost in the fire. I think we may be able to help you with some clothes for your sons. My wife Rose may have kept some of our son's clothing. Let me check with her." He left the room and returned with Rose carrying a stack of clothing in her arms. Her face was bright as she announced "I always wondered why I kept these clothes after our son moved to Montana. Now I know why! I even have some of his baby clothes packed away. If you have need for baby clothes, just let me know!"

Perry perked up at Rose's comment about baby clothes. "As a matter of fact, we are expecting a new baby. We may take you up on that kind offer, Rose. My Jennie may need some help with the birth of the child. Is that something you can help us with?" Perry asked excitedly. "Mrs. Duncan, I have helped with the birth of many of the babies born in Sheridan for 30 years. I would be pleased to be with you when the time comes," she smiled as she looked at Jennie.

When Rose spoke directly to Jennie about helping her with the birth, she bristled. "I have managed to give birth to four children on my own. Thank you, Mrs. Shenk," she snapped. Awkward silence settled heavy in the room until Perry chirped up. "Thank you for the clothes, Rose. We will see both of you in two weeks."

Stiff necked, Jennie turned and left the building carrying the stack of clothing for her sons. Looking back to tip his hat, Perry followed slowly behind Jennie out the heavy wooden front door.

Perry lifted himself to the wagon and peeked into the wagon to see his sons sitting in their underclothes. "Well, look at you! he called out to the boys. Today is your lucky day. Mrs. Shenk has given us some clothes for you to wear until we are able to buy new things." 'Jennie, hand me those clothes", he called down to his wife still standing outside. Jennie shoved the stack of clothing on to the seat of the wagon. Looking at Jennie curiously, he took the clothing and handed it into the wagon to his sons. Anxiously, they clutched the clothing and began holding the shirts and trousers up to see which ones would fit them.

Closing the curtain, Perry looked at Jennie and asked her in a hushed tone, "What is going on with you Jennie? I know you had a rough night but you seem to be angry with everyone this morning." Glaring at Perry, she hissed "How dare you make plans for that woman to help me give birth without my permission, and to take clothing from her like we are some charity case." Perry shouted back, "That's enough, Jennie. If Sheridan is going to be our home, you best be trying to get along with folks here. These people have been very good to us in our circumstances. Climb up here on the wagon. I am driving us back to the property! We'll make a short stop at the Mercantile to find bedrolls and shoes for our sons."

As the wagon pulled up to the Mercantile on Railway Street, Perry instructed Jennie to stay on the wagon with the boys. "I will be in the mercantile for just a few minutes. You don't need to come in with me", he said without looking at Jennie. After Perry had disappeared in the door of the building, Jennie pulled the curtain aside and looked at her sons seated quietly in the back. "I suppose you are all happy with your hand- me -down clothing now. You weren't happy with the clothes your own mother made. You all look like you just got off work on the railroad in those old scruffy clothes." She quickly jerked the curtain closed without giving her sons a chance to respond.

Perry came from the mercantile with a pile of tied up bed-rolls and three pair of western boots tied in a bundle for his sons. Instead of climbing on to the wagon from the front, he carried the pack to the back of the wagon and passed the items through to his sons. Jesse called out, "Pa, thank you! These are the best boots we have ever had!" As he walked to the front of the wagon, Perry heard his sons' squeals of delight coming from inside the wagon as they tried on their new boots.

"How in God's name did you pay for all those items, Perry Duncan? Jennie sternly asked. Perry looked at Jennie and smiled. "I put them on a ticket, Jennie. I told them I would be back in two weeks to pay for them. They know where to find me."

Perry and Jennie rode side by side on the wagon seat for two hours without speaking to each other. Perry whistled as they churned down the bumpy trail, guiding the horse team with one hand. Jennie sat straight backed with her head turned away from Perry.

The evening sun nudged up against the mountains to the west as the Duncan's arrived at their campsite. When the horses halted, Perry jumped from the wagon and began unhitching the team with his good hand. "When did these horses last have water, Jennie?" Still seated on the wagon, she looked at Perry in dismay. "I'm not sure, Perry. We were too busy and I forgot to water them", she said fretfully. Perry called out, "Jesse, come out here and help me get these horses to water. They're foaming at the mouth from thirst." The curtain flung open as Jesse jumped on to the seat next to Jennie. His new boots flopped on his feet as he jumped off the wagon to the ground. Handing a rein to Jesse, Perry grinned at Jesse as they led the horses to the creek for water. "You'll grow into those boots before long, son. You best be wearing an extra pair of socks so you don't get all blistered up. You need to tell your brothers the same thing. I can't have all three of you limping around. I'm going to need all of you to help me getting our house built." "Our socks got burned up in the fire too, Pa", Jesse mumbled. Taking a deep breath, Perry said. "Your Ma can show you and your brothers how to wrap your feet in some old feed sack fabric until we can get you some new socks. Your Ma is good at making do." Jesse answered his Pa, "Ma said we looked like old railroad workers in these clothes, Pa. She didn't like that we're wearing someone else's clothes. She wants us to wear Lizzy's clothes." Stooping down, Perry grasped Jesse's shoulders and said, "Your Ma just wants the best for all of you. She means well. We have to be patient with her while we are living in the wagons. We need to get her house built so she feels she has a home to live in."

As Perry and Jesse arrived back at camp with the horses, the smell of food cooking filled the summer evening air. Vere and Ike carried burlap bags of vegetables and potatoes from the wagon to Jennie as she turned a slab of salted meat on the cast iron griddle. "Sure smells good, Jennie", Perry called as he tied up the horses to the back wagon. Approaching Jennie, Perry quietly asked her where the brown bottle of medicine was. "It's in the wagon box next to the horse blanket, Perry", she said as she looked into his face. She could see that his pain was breaking through after the long hours of traveling from Sheridan. Disappearing into the wagon for a few minutes, Perry emerged and sat on the seat resting his bandaged arm on the sideboard.

Jesse climbed on to the wagon seat next to Perry. "Pa, is your broken arm hurting? Can I get another whiskey bottle for you, Pa?" "No, son, I'm doing better now. Dr, Shenk gave me some medicine to take and it is working fine", he said faintly. Shifting his weight on the seat, Perry leaned back and closed his eyes.

Jennie called out to announce that dinner was ready. Still seated next to his Pa on the wagon, Jesse nudged Perry to let him know it was time to eat. Perry opened his eyes slightly, then closed them and shook his head. "Pa doesn't want to eat, Ma", he called out. Vere and Ike ran from the tall grass near the draw.

"Jesse, come down and get some dinner. I'll sit with your Pa for a spell till he is ready to eat", Jennie said. After handing her sons their plates of food, she climbed onto the wagon and whispered in Perry's ear. "Perry, you need to eat something. I know you don't feel hungry but you need to eat while I have some hot food here". Rolling his head from side to side back against the canvas cover, Perry responded weakly, "No Jennie. If I eat something, I'll be sick." Grasping his hand, Jennie led him inside the wagon and urged him to lie down. Covering him with the horse blanket, she kissed his forehead and left the wagon.

Perry slept soundly in spite of the racket from the Duncan boys getting settled into the other wagon for the night. Jennie untied the new bedrolls and spread them out inside the wagon. After leaving the wagon, there were loud arguments as to which bedroll belonged to whom. Jennie put an end to the disagreements just by opening the curtain and looking inside. The Duncan boys' eyes widened as they saw their mother's face suddenly appear in the separated curtain, and the quarrelling instantly ceased. As Jennie tidied up the campsite for the night, she overheard whispered accusations coming from within the boys' wagon. The hour was too late and her body was too exhausted to intervene further.

CHAPTER 41

RED FEATHER ARRIVES

Before daybreak, the high-pitched sound of yipping coyotes close to camp awoke Jennie. Lying in the darkness, she remembered the many nights of listening to the coyotes on Cherry Creek. Every remembrance of Cherry Creek still brought memories of her precious Lizzy. She understood that she could never really replace the child but now she had the hope of having a new baby girl to hold. She recently felt the unborn baby moving inside her womb, just as Lizzy did. The thrill of that sensation brought hope to Jennie.

Perry jolted awake, startling Jennie as she lay beside him. "Jennie, what is that noise?" he yelled. "Its okay, Perry. Just coyotes". Propping himself up, he felt around the bedroll for Jennie. "I'm here, Perry. Go back to sleep. It isn't time to get up yet". Jennie gently nudged Perry back down and stroked his arm. "Jennie, I need some pain medicine. I am hurting pretty badly right now. Can you get it for me?" Jennie opened the curtain and hooked it to let in moonlight. She carefully opened the wagon box, grasped the bottle and pulled the cork. Handing it to Perry, she said, "Perry, go easy with this medicine. It dampens your appetite and you need to eat something in the morning. That bone won't heal unless you eat something. You get one swig, that's it", she said. Taking the bottle, Perry took a long swig and lay back down. Jennie listened. Minutes later Perry's breathing slowed.

Unable to get back to sleep, Jennie lay listening to the sounds of the night. Oddly, the coyotes hushed. The night air felt eerily stagnant. Lifting her head from the featherbed, Jennie sensed something peculiar. Suddenly she heard grass rustling just outside the wagon. In that same moment, a heavy thud shook the wagon. Bolting up, she reached under the wagon box and wrapped her fingers around her gun. Crawling to the curtain, she cautiously opened it just enough to see if any silhouettes were in view. Nothing appeared out of place. Just under the front seat of the wagon, out of her sight, she heard the brittle grass crunching. Spinning her head to Perry, she realized that Perry was helplessly drugged by the medicine from the brown bottle. He would be of no assistance if she needed it. Crouching on her quivering knees, Jennie felt panic rising to her neck. It could be one of her sons who left the wagon and got sidetracked in the darkness. As the panic reached high pitch, she bellowed "Who is it?" The grass rustled again. Perry lay motionless, unconscious of the events around him. Unwilling to wait for a response, Jennie grasped the lantern, lit it with shaking hands and forcefully threw the curtain open. Her fear simmered up inside her to boiling anger. Jumping off the wagon with her gun in one hand and the swinging lantern in the other, she landed hard on the ground with her teeth clenched. Swirling around, she daringly shoved the lantern under the wagon seat to see what hid there.

Peering back at Jennie, she saw the eyes of a frightened young man holding his hands up to his face as if to protect himself. Stepping back, Jennie called out "Who are you and what do you want?" A weak whispered response came from the young man, "Please help." Stepping closer to the wagon, Jennie hung the lantern on the edge of the seat and looked closer. She somehow knew that face. "Come out now", she called out. Lying on his back, the man slid out from under the wagon. Holding the lantern up, Jennie saw that the side of his face was covered in dried blood. Tears dripped from his eyes. Jennie laid the gun on the seat and held her hand out to help him get to his feet. As he stood teetering in front of her, Jennie put her hands on her head. "My God ! It's you? You are the Indian boy with the red feathered horse?" The young man nodded his head. "What has happened to you? Let me help you". Limping beside Jennie, the boy held her arm as she led him to a stump near the campfire. Wincing as he lowered himself to sit, he spoke softly. "I am Crow Indian. My fellow tribesmen were killed by outlaws yesterday. I am left alone." Stooping down to look into his face, Jennie put her hand on his shoulder. "We will help you. What is your name?" "Red Feather", he said.

Jesse called to his mother from his wagon. "Ma, who are you talking to?"

Everything is okay, Jesse. Go back to sleep. It isn't time to get up yet."

Jennie built a fire to warm some water for Red Feather. She gently wiped the blood from his face and warmed broth for him to drink. The young man sat quietly as Jennie tended to his wounds. From her wagon, she brought a vile of the willow juice she had made for Perry. "Drink a bit of this willow juice and it will make you feel better" she urged him.

Yellow rays of light burst over the eastern horizon. Lying on the ground next to the fire, Red Feather slept after drinking the broth Jennie made for him. She covered him with a horse blanket and crept back into the wagon to check on Perry. Perry stirred as she crawled up beside him. Opening his eyes, he said to Jennie "Is it time to get up, Jennie?" Jennie quickly replied "Perry, remember me telling you about the young Indian man who helped me on this trip? He is here at camp with us Perry."

"What? Jennie, what are you saying?" "He came in the night, badly injured. His fellow tribesmen were killed and he was left for dead but managed to escape and found his way to our wagon." Brushing the hair from his face, Perry sat up and looked around the wagon. "Jennie is it safe for him to be here?" He whispered.

"I don't care if it is safe or not, Perry. He is here and I am going to take care of him. He took care of me when I needed help. I have no idea how he found us, especially in the dark, but I will not send him away". Perry looked at Jennie and smiled weakly at her indignant posture. Grasping her hand he said "Mrs. Duncan, I know it would be foolish of me to try and change your mind about this young man. If you trust him, I'll trust him".

Looking into Perry's bloodshot eyes, Jennie said "I can hardly believe that this young man found our wagon, Perry. It doesn't make sense except that I think he was meant to find us. It doesn't make sense at all. Some things are meant, Perry." Pulling her hand from Perry's grasp, she left the wagon.

As Jennie stepped outside the wagon, she saw that Red Feather had awakened and was limping from camp. She called out to him "Wait, Red Feather! You don't have to leave here. We will take care of you till you are strong enough to leave." Turning around to Jennie, the young man hesitated, and then spoke. "I don't want trouble for you, woman". "Call me Jennie", she said loudly as she approached him. Touching his arm, she continued, "My husband is seriously injured and I need help building our house. I will feed you. You stay and help me build the house". Looking down to the ground, he said "I never build house but I will help you, Mrs. Jennie".

As Jennie and Red Feather turned around and headed back to camp, Jennie saw the Duncan boys hiding behind her wagon peeking around the corner. She called the boys to her. They approached their mother cautiously. "I want you to meet Red Feather. He will be helping us to build the house" she said confidently. Looking to each other first, then to Red Feather, the Duncan boys nodded.

Perry Duncan sluggishly inched down the side of the wagon to drop his feet to the ground. Holding on to the side board, he scrutinized the situation as Jennie, Red Feather and his sons walked toward camp.

Jennie moved swiftly toward Perry with Red Feather walking behind her like a reluctant shadow. When she reached Perry, she looked around to see the young man standing several yards behind her. Jennie motioned for him to join her and Perry. Walking guardedly forward, he stood straight with his head high. "Perry, this is Red Feather. He is the young man who helped me when I was lost on the prairie. He has agreed to stay and help us get the house built. We will feed him and give him shelter", she announced forcefully. Perry extended his hand to Red Feather, "Thank you for agreeing to stay with us, Red Feather. And thank you for helping my wife. We need your help and we welcome you." Red Feather tentatively extended his strong sinewy hand to Perry. Huddled close together, the Duncan boys watched their parents and Red Feather from a distance.

Jennie set about preparing breakfast for her group. Red Feather hovered close as she cooked over the cast iron pan. "How did you find us, Red Feather? I thought I saw your horse in Casper when we came through there. It was outside the Dispensary. Was that your horse?" He nodded. "Why were you there? Jennie stopped and made eye contact with him. "I was there with Great Wolf. He was injured by a blow to his head. The wound would not stop bleeding. He was not thinking right." Jennie swallowed hard. "Was he your friend, Red Feather?" she asked slowly. Red Feather blurted out, "Not my friend, Mrs. Jennie! Great Wolf not a good warrior. He treat people bad." Jennie continued to inquire about Great Wolf. "Where is Great Wolf now?" Red Feather looked Jennie in the eye and said, "Great Wolf is gone. He died from white man gun. He tried to kill white man. He tried to kill you, Mrs. Jennie".

Jennie dropped the heavy metal spoon into the pan with a loud clank. Her eyes widened as she looked into Red Feather's face and said in horror, "You are saying that Great Wolf was the man who tried to attack me? Were you there with him?"

"Great Wolf try to kill you more than one time, Mrs. Jennie. I stop him."

"Why did you stay with him? Jennie asked. "I stay with him because he was my elder, my teacher" he responded. "I must stay with my teacher. Now my teacher is gone so I am alone." Jennie's eyes softened as she asked Red Feather, "Where is your mother?" "My mother is gone. She was old and tired. She no longer had eyes to see the sunrise and sunset. Her time was to go." Jennie's first inclination was to wrap the young man in her arms but realized that was not the Indian tradition. She smiled and said, "You were a good son to her, Red Feather. You honor her. So, how did you come to find us, Red Feather", Jennie continued. "Great Wolf followed your wagons and watched. After he was killed, I followed your wagon tracks. I was injured and alone and didn't know where to go. I believe my mother's strong spirit led me here", he said.

Gathering around the morning fire, the Duncan family and Red Feather ate a hearty breakfast. Enthusiastic and light hearted, the group set about going to the new home site to begin work on the log home. Perry Duncan led the way on his horse, riding with one hand clutching the reins. Jennie drove the wagon to the site with the Duncan boys and Red Feather. Upon arrival at the site, Jennie asked the young Indian man, "Where is your horse with the red feathers in the mane?" He responded despondently "My horse ran away when Great Wolf was killed. I searched for many days to find him. I think white men have him now." Jennie's eyes flashed as she said, "We will find that horse, Red Feather". I believe he will show up somewhere around here. He knows his master."

CHAPTER 42

COMMENCING CONSTRUCTION

S tanding at the foot of the pile of logs at the new home site, Perry stared up at the roughhewn stacked pine remembering how they rumbled down upon him, twisting and snapping his arm. Stomping his foot, he turned to find his family and Red Feather watching. "Let's get started with this project", he yelled to the group. "Bring me a rope". Jennie pointed out to Jesse where the ropes were stored in the side wagon box. Gathering a heavy loop of rope, he struggled to drag it to Perry.

Red Feather ran to assist Jesse, lifting the rope from the ground and delivering it to Perry. "We're going to need more rope to get more than one log moving in succession. We'll be working an assembly line of moving these logs. Jennie, you will not be lifting any heavy logs. Do you understand? Jesse, you will be helping Red Feather drag the logs. Ike and Vere will be gathering dried grass to use as chinking. Jennie, I need you to mix the dried grass with dirt and water to make the chinking to put in between the logs.

We will start with the first row of logs on the flat ground and work up to more rows".

Every member of the group scattered to begin their designated task. Jennie gave the youngest boys a burlap sack to gather the dried grass. She retrieved a large metal basin from the wagon and a stoneware jug to gather water from the stream. Perry, perched wrapped the rope around the end of each log. The veins and muscles in his arm strained as he knotted the rope firmly in place.

Jesse and Red Feather drug the logs one by one to the flat site and placed them in a rectangular shape on the ground. When the first row was set in place, Perry left his post at the stack of wood to show Red Feather how to bind the logs together at the corners. By late afternoon, five rows of logs were in place. As the group stood together to behold the beginnings of the new Duncan home, Perry looked to his wife. Her skirt, caked with wet gray mud, hung heavily on her body. Chinking mud had worked deep into her fingernails. The flesh on her hands was raw from the chafing of the dried grass and thick coarse dirt. Weary from the day's work, Jennie noticed her husband looking at her. Furtively, she buried her hands in the deep dark pockets of her skirt.

The days were scorching hot and the nights were short for the builders of the Duncan home. Routines of the project became more precise as the days passed. After the walls were completed, Jennie, precariously positioned high on the brace logs with her husband, braced the logs in place as Perry hammered with long flat head iron nails. Red Feather, climbing up a homemade ladder of tree branches, pushed the logs to the roof with his strong powerful arms. Perry retrieved the logs with his one strong hand. Working late into the August evening, the roof was completed on the eleventh day of construction.

The log home consisted of one large open room inside with a dirt floor. The young Duncan boys were instructed to gather rocks from the small creek near the house to use in the construction of a fireplace. Carrying and stacking rocks for several days outside the building became a competition to determine which of the Duncan boys could amass the largest pile. The youngest Duncan boy's pile of rocks was woefully small in comparison with his older brothers. Red Feather noticed the youngster's struggle to carry enough rocks from the creek to increase his pile size. Sneaking to the home site early one morning to add rocks to Vere's pile, Red Feather doubled the size of young Vere's pile without revealing his participation. When the group arrived at the home site after Red Feather's secret visit, Vere's eyes grew wide in disbelief as he approached his majestic rock pile. Jennie knowingly looked to the young Indian man and smiled.

Hard work continued on the Duncan home in the warm August sun. Red Feather was a quick study and became Perry's right hand man. Stopping only for food and water breaks, the group made abundant progress every day. Perry still took swigs of the medicine in the brown bottle throughout the day.

Rocks gathered by the Duncan boys were stacked and mortared to form a spacious fireplace and chimney in the center of the north wall of the home. "We'll get to Sheridan to purchase glass for windows in the home", Perry whispered to Jennie as they stood admiring their home. "We'll put a window looking to the west so you'll have a view of the sunset, Jennie. We'll also put one on the east side so you can see the sunrise as well."

Jennie's unborn child grew and kicked as the days passed. Her long cotton skirt had become snugger across her stomach. On a trip to Sheridan for Perry's final visit with Dr. Shenk for an exam of his arm, the doctor gave Perry the news that he could begin using the arm for the construction project. After the exam, the doctor turned to Jennie and asked how she was doing with the new baby on the way. Jennie's attitude toward Mrs. Shenk had softened. She asked Dr. Shenk to request that his wife be present at the birth of the baby.

Leaving the room, Dr. Shenk returned with his wife. "Mrs. Duncan, I will be honored to assist you with the birth of your new baby", she said as she approached Jennie holding her arms open to Jennie. Jennie welcomed Mrs. Shenk's warm embrace. Smiling at Jennie, she said "How soon should we expect this child to arrive, Mrs. Duncan?" Her cheeks blushed pink as she responded, "As soon as our house is completed."

Before leaving Sheridan, Perry drove the wagon to the glass shop near the railroad tracks. A man in the shop told Perry that they had made two extra windows for the Sheridan Inn after the fire. The two new windows were available to purchase that day. Noticing that the windows were larger than he planned for the home, Perry called Jennie to get her approval of the larger size windows. Her eyes were wide with wonder as she gazed at the beautiful windows. The shop merchant told Perry he could have the windows for 'next to nothing" since they were made for the Inn and wouldn't be used. "Consider them sold!" Perry shouted. Perry and Red Feather loaded the windows in the back of the wagon next to the Duncan boys. "You boys be careful not to lean on these new windows. They are for our new home', Perry instructed.

As the wagon pulled away from the glass shop, Perry threw his arms in the air. "Look Jennie, I can install these windows with both arms when we get back!"

Red Feather and the Duncan boys rode quietly in the back of the wagon with the new windows propped up beside them. Pulling a long piece of twine from his tunic pocket, Red Feather showed the boys some twine knots and finger games. Jesse caught on first and engaged his brothers in the string games with Red Feather. Laughter from the back of the wagon prompted Jennie to turn around to look inside at the uncommon passengers. Surprised by Jennie's quick jerk of the wagon curtain, Red Feather's eyes grew wide with concern. Jennie smiled and nodded her head.

Once back at the home site, the Duncan's and Red Feather filed out of the wagon and approached the standing empty shell of the new home. Perry signaled to Red Feather to help unload the heavy windows. As the windows were placed in the home near the location of where they would be installed, Jennie's face beamed with joy as she envisioned the views of the hills and mountains she would have when they were installed. Standing beside her, Perry and Red Feather watched Jennie's reaction. Jennie turned to Perry and wrapped her arms around his neck. She then embraced Red Feather in the same way. Red Feather stood straight backed showing only fear as Jennie embraced him. He immediately backed away from Jennie and left the building. "I guess I shouldn't have done that", she said as she looked at Perry. "He'll be fine, Jennie. He isn't used to a beautiful woman grabbing and hugging him", Perry winked as he grinned at his wife.

With a few hours of daylight left, Perry set about chiseling out an outline of where the new windows would be set. Eventually, Red Feather returned to the house to assist Perry. From the corner of his eye, he watched Jennie as she busied herself preparing food for an evening meal for the family. "We'll have to saw out these logs once the outline is completed" he said to Red Feather as they took turns pounding the outline into the logs. Red Feather's arms were stronger and steadier as he pounded the pine logs along the outline Perry had drawn. Resting nearby, Perry massaged his arm near the purple scar on his arm.

As the sun set below the hills to the west, Jennie called the family to dinner. Perry touched Red Feather on the shoulder to signal him to come to dinner. Startled by Perry's touch, Red Feather dropped the heavy metal chisel on the ground and swung around. "It's okay, boy. I'm sorry I scared you. It's time to go and eat something", Perry said. Red Feather followed Perry to the wagon camp site and sat with the Duncan boys. He glanced up at Jennie only briefly as she spooned some food onto his plate. "You must be starved, Red Feather. You have been working nonstop for hours", she said as she served food to him. "Thank you, Mrs. Jennie" was his quiet response. Cocking her head to the side, she looked at Red Feather and said. "You can call me Jennie, Red Feather".

The family chattered about the installation of the new windows. Perry told the boys that more chinking would have to be made to put around the new windows when they were put in. "You will need to gather more dried grass and smooth dirt in the morning so we can seal the windows. I don't want your Ma to have to do all the mixing this time. You saw how she did it and this time I want you boys to mix it up. I will need Red Feather and your Ma to help me hold the windows in place to nail them up while you are mixing the mortar.

"Pa, can we take our bedrolls into the house and sleep in there tonight?" Jesse pleaded. Perry pondered the question and replied "We don't have a door on the house yet. No telling what critters might join you in there." Red Feather quickly responded, "I watch over boys, Mr. Duncan". Looking to Jennie, Perry waited for her reaction. She said "As long as Red Feather will be with them, I don't see why they can't stay in the house tonight." Jumping up with their arms in the air, the Duncan boys cheered their Ma's approval. Jennie looked to Red Feather and smiled. "Under your watchful eye, our sons will be safe, Red Feather. Thank you for this." Red Feather, still seated on the ground, looked up into Jennie's eyes and nodded.

The Duncan boys jumped from their places at the meal to retrieve their bedrolls. Shaking her head, Jennie questioned, "Why would anyone want to sleep on the cold hard ground when they could be warm in the wagon?" "Adventure, Jennie. This is high adventure for the boys", Perry whispered. Perry rose from his place to retrieve an old canvas tarp from the wagon. Carrying it to Red Feather, he told him to cover the ground for the boys to place under their bedrolls. After Perry left the house, Jennie arrived with a lantern and handed it to Red Feather. As Red Feather grasped the lantern, Jennie's fingers gently brushed against his hand. In the glow of the warm lantern light, Red Feather looked into Jennie's soft blue eyes. Something stirred inside of him that he had never experienced. He remembered her warm body against his chest as she hugged him earlier in the day. His heart raced as he turned away from Jennie abruptly. The lantern swung wildly in his hand causing the light from the lantern to whimsically dance across the log walls. "Red Feather, is everything okay with you? Are you feeling well?' Jennie called out to him. "Yes, Mrs. Jennie", he managed to blurt out. As she turned to leave the building, she looked over her shoulder to see the young man's eyes following her.

Shaking off the peculiar feeling she had from the lantern encounter with Red Feather, Jennie pulled the warm comforter over herself in the wagon. Snoring noisily after taking a swig of the medicine, Perry slept. Jennie listened as her sons whispered animatedly into the night. She wondered how Red Feather could sleep with the babbling of the Duncan boys nearby. As the night grew deeper, Jennie slept, as well.

Awakened by shuffling noises outside her wagon, Jennie crawled to the front of the wagon to investigate. Crisp morning air surged through the opened canvas curtain as she quietly pulled it. Focusing her eyes in the shadowy light, she saw Red Feather stacking wood on the fire. Leaning back on her heels, she sat in wonder about the young Indian man whom they welcomed into their lives. In a time when there was so much antagonism between the white settlers and the Indians, this young man had no malice in his heart for either side. Jennie expected him to be gone at any time now that Perry's arm was healing and he was able to work on the Duncan home without assistance. Still, he chose to stay with the Duncan family. She could only guess his age. She believed that he was probably in his twenties, a few years younger than Jennie. He was strong, both physically and mentally, yet he had uncommon compassion and concern for her and the Duncan family. Without disturbing Perry, she quickly dressed herself and left the wagon. As she stepped out, Red Feather startled at her appearance.

Hastily, he stood up and apologized to Jennie for waking her. "Mrs. Jennie, I didn't mean to wake you. Your sons are still asleep in the house but I was awake and …" "Red Feather, don't apologize. I was awake. How did the boys sleep last night? Did they keep you awake all night with their silly ramblings?" "No, Mrs. Jennie, everyone sleep well."

Jennie motioned for Red Feather to take a seat next to her on the old cottonwood stump. "Come sit next to me. I have some questions for you, Red Feather", she said.

The young man warily seated himself next to Jennie. She placed her warm hand on his and squeezed gently. "I know you appreciate having a place to live and feel safe with us, Red Feather. I also know that since your horse is gone, you have no way to leave right now. I want you to know you are welcome to stay with us as long as you wish but if you want to leave, I will help you find another horse." Gazing down at Jennie's hand on his, Red Feather slipped his fingers around Jennie's hand. "I love you, Mrs. Jennie. You are beautiful woman. I want to help Mr. Duncan to take care of you." Slowly and deliberately, Jennie drew her hand from Red Feather's grasp. Searching his face, she tried to interpret what the young man was saying. "You mean that you love me like you loved your mother? She queried. "Yes, like my mother. She was like you, Mrs. Jennie". Breathing a sigh of relief, Jennie jumped to her feet. "Young man, you are surely hungry. Get that fire stoked and I'll get some breakfast started." Red Feather interrupted Jennie's orders. "Mrs. Jennie, there is something I must say. My father was white man. He was killed because he loved my mother. I do not want harm to come to you because of me." Jennie stood riveted at Red Feather's confession. Reaching out to him, she wrapped her arms around him and held him closely. Resting her chin on his shoulder, she whispered, "Thank you for telling me this. Everything will be okay and now we will take care of you as you have taken care of us."

As Jennie busied herself around camp, her mind raced through the scenario that Red Feather had just posed to her. Somehow things seemed different now that she knew that his father was a white man. She had a realization that the young man was trapped between two cultures and didn't know which one he should claim as his own. It didn't really matter to Jennie that Red Feather's father was a white man but she could tell that it mattered to him. He held the secret close. Jennie suspected that he had told nobody about it including the tribesmen he traveled with. She turned around from the wagon box to see him crouched near the fire pit. For the first time, she focused on his facial features. She always viewed him as a handsome young man. His deep hazel eyes and striking black hair framed high cheekbones and a wide bright smile. Shrugging her shoulders, she thought, "So what, nothing is different now. He is still Red Feather, the compassionate young man who saved my life many times over."

Red Feather caught Jennie observing him. Turning away from her view, he lowered his head in regret about telling Jennie his deepest secret. Quickly jumping to his feet, he turned and approached Jennie. "Mrs. Jennie, don't be afraid of what I say to you. If you want me to leave this place, I will go."

She took his hands in hers and said "You never have to leave this place, Red Feather. You leave only when you want to go. That is my final word on this subject."

Staggering from the wagon, Perry pushed the hair from his face and yawned. "I guess a man can't get any extra sleep around here", he called out. "Seems like I just bedded down and it's time to get up again." Red Feather turned abruptly to Perry. "Mr. Duncan, I will start work on the house. If you need rest, I can do work". Perry walked to Red Feather and rested his hand on the young man's shoulder. "You have been right beside me all this time getting this house built, Son. We'll work together. We are almost finished. And one more thing, can I call you Red? Or should I call you Feather?" The young man looked at Perry in inquisitiveness. "Mr. Duncan, you called me Son. I like for you to call me Son." "Consider it done, Son. I like that name. How about Sonny?" Red Feather smiled and repeated "Sonny". "Yes, Mr. Duncan, I like Sonny." Perry put his hand out for a handshake. Red Feather extended his hand to

Perry. "Now, here is the thing, Sonny. You call me Perry from now on, Okay?" Watching the exchange between Perry and Red Feather, Jennie nodded. If only Perry knew what Red Feather had told her this morning about his father being a white man? She knew that this meant a lot to Red Feather to have Perry call him Son.

After breakfast the group set about to get the windows installed in the Duncan home. Perry lifted a heavy metal hand saw and handed it to Red Feather. "My arm isn't strong enough to start this project, Sonny. If you get the cut started, I can take over when you need a break." Red Feather took the saw and examined it in wonder. Breaking out in laughter, Perry reached out for the saw and demonstrated to Sonny how to use it. He placed the saw blade into the chiseled open space and showed Sonny how to begin the process of sawing through the logs under the open notch. "Sonny, you got this thing figured out", Perry called out as he watched the young man saw through the logs with vigor. The fragrance of warm pine pitch filled the air as saw dust floated through the air under the window opening. In less than an hour, Sonny had sawed through the logs to complete the first window opening. Perry called out to Jennie to help hold the new window in place. "Jennie, it's time to nail the window up!" Jennie came running from the field where she was helping the boys gather dried grass for the chinking around the window. As she ran from the field, she braced her bouncing protuberant stomach. Breathless, she arrived with a wide smile on her pink lips. "It's beautiful" she called out as she looked through the open doorway.

Perry and Sonny held the window up to show Jennie. Throwing her arms in the air she yelled "Yes, Yes! It fits perfectly!"

"Come over here, Jennie. Brace the window while Sonny holds it in place." While Perry nailed the window in place, Jennie watched Sonny's arms shudder under the weight of the heavy window. She shifted her stance to steady the window with her shoulder for more support. Looking into the young man's face, she whispered, "Sonny, are you doing okay?" The young man's face beamed as he said "Yes, Mrs. Jennie. Uh, Yes, Jennie. I am strong."

The window fit almost perfectly in the open space. Pounding furiously, Perry nailed the window in place. Standing back the three admired the new glass. Tiny bands of daylight beamed through the sides of the window frame. Pointing to the light, Perry said to Jennie, "This is where the extra chinking will have to be put in, Jennie."

CHAPTER 43

A CHILD ARRIVES

Twirling around to leave the house, Jennie bent over and grasped her stomach. A shrill cry emanated from her as she collapsed to the floor. Perry rushed to her. Kneeling beside her, Perry wrapped his arms around her. "Jennie, what is it?" "It's the baby, Perry. I think the baby is coming." Helping Jennie to her feet, Perry swept her up in his arms and carried her to the wagon. Lifting her onto the wagon, he said "Jennie, I want you to rest for a bit. If you think the baby is coming right away, I will either send for Dr. Shenk's wife or take you in to Sheridan. What do you think?"

"Give me a few minutes, Perry. I might have just moved the wrong way and pulled a muscle or twisted too quickly. I will rest a bit and see if I have any cause to believe the baby is coming. Right now, I'm not having any pain." Lifting Jennie's hand to his face, Perry kissed it and stepped away. Looking back to his wife, he pushed his hair from his face and ambled around to the other side of the wagon where Sonny stood. "Jennie may have to go into Sheridan if this baby is coming, Sonny. I would have to leave the boys here with you." The young man said in urgent tone, "Mr. Duncan, I go into to Sheridan and bring doctor to Mrs. Jennie".

With his hands on his hips, Perry looked to the wagon and considered Sonny's offer. "That might be the better option, Sonny. I will check on Jennie's condition in a few minutes and see if she thinks the baby is coming today. Gather a horse and get it ready just in case I need you to ride into Sheridan." Sonny quickly turned and ran toward the horse pasture.

Kicking the dirt under his feet, Perry looked back to the wagon where Jennie rested. In Cherry Creek, a neighbor woman came to help Jennie with the birth of her sons. She had since died and knew nothing of Jennie's obsession of raising the boys as daughters. Perry pondered this birth outcome. In Cherry Creek, they had a warm home for the newborns. He was troubled that Jennie may have to give birth in a sooty wagon.

Sonny rushed up behind Perry with a horse ready to go. As if being awakened from a sound sleep, Perry jerked around in surprise at Sonny's arrival. "I will go check on Jennie now to see if she thinks the baby is on the way", he said.

Climbing up on the wagon, Perry slowly pulled the curtain aside and looked in at Jennie. Her eyes were closed. Jennie she was sleeping soundly. Gently closing the curtain, Perry left the wagon and approached Sonny. "Jennie is sleeping now, Sonny. If she was in any distress, she would not be sleeping. Keep the horse close by and I'll check her again in a while. We might as well get started on getting that second window put in. Now that you know how to do it, can you get started with cutting the opening?" "Sure, Mr. Perry. I'll get started."

Pacing inside the house Perry stopped in front of the newly placed glass window and peered outside to the gently rolling hills.

He loved the thought of living in this quiet serene location nestled in the green hills near Sheridan. The house wasn't ready for a new baby yet. This baby needed to wait just a day or two for Perry to have the house ready.

A loud cry from Jennie shook Perry from his daydream. Sonny dropped the saw and ran to side of the wagon. Perry was a step behind and bounded onto the wagon in a single leap. Throwing the curtain open, he found Jennie lying propped on her elbows. Her face was flushed red. She called out "Perry, the baby is coming now!" Perry turned and called out to Sonny, "Get Dr. Shenk, Sonny. This baby wants to be born." Jennie shrieked, "No, I can't wait for any doctor. I mean the baby is coming NOW. Reach into this side box and get the clean white fabric and place them under me. Do it now, Perry!" Perry's hands shook as he opened the box of fabric. Spreading the fresh linen under Jennie's trembling legs, he calmly spoke to Jennie. "Jennie, what do I need to do now? She threw her head back and bellowed, "Perry, I can't do this!" Perry grasped a pillow and placed it under Jennie's head. He took her face in his hands and said, "Jennie, you can do this. I am here to help you. Try to calm down and relax." "Relax? You want me to relax, Perry? Are you insane? Another labor pain struck Jennie. Her scream echoed in the valley. The young Duncan boys circled the wagon calling out to Perry. "Pa, what is wrong with Ma? Pa, what should we do"? Perry called out, "Get me a cool clean rag soaked in water. Everything is okay, sons. Your Ma is having the baby."

Over and over, pain gripped Jennie's body. Arching her back, the veins in her neck protruded as she grit her teeth, trying to keep from screaming. Perry squeezed her hand as she progressed through the pains.

It seemed like hours had passed. After a particularly strong labor pain had eased, Jennie propped herself up to look around the wagon. "Perry, you need to get a clean knife blade and twine in here. Tell the boys that I am going to be fine. I don't want them afraid of what is happening here." "Boys, I need you to gather some of those willow leaves for your Ma. Go now." Throwing the cool wet rag toward Perry, the three boys turned from the wagon and ran toward the draw. Jumping off the wagon, Perry noticed that Sonny and the horse were gone. He ran to the side box. Thrashing through the box, he pulled out one of his sharp hunting knives and a ball of twine. When he got back into the wagon Jennie instructed him to clean the knife with some of the medicine that Dr. Shenk had given him for his arm pain. After he cleaned the knife, he held the bottle up and asked Jennie if she wanted a sip. "Jennie, take a small sip of this just to help you through this." Jennie grasped the bottle and sipped a tiny amount just before another pain overtook her again. Perry had been in the area when the other children were born but he never had to assist in the birthing process. His face furrowed in fear as he watched Jennie writhe in pain. After Jennie quieted down, he yelled to her, "What now, Jennie? What should I do now?

Lifting her head off the pillow, Jennie said quietly, "Perry, you need to check to see if the baby's head is starting to show. Just as you have helped many heifers calve, you need to check to see if the baby is coming out yet." Perry carefully lifted Jennie's skirt from her legs and told her to bend her knees. She followed his orders. "Yes! I see the baby's head, Jennie. The baby is coming, Jennie!" "Jennie's face was dripping in perspiration as she said, "When the next pain comes Perry, I am going to push. Place your hands under me so that you can guide the baby out gently." She propped herself up on her elbows again and yelled "NOW,

Perry.! Her loud shrill scream pierced Perry's ears. He knelt down and held his trembling hands under the baby's head as it slowly emerged from Jennie. When the baby's body had completely emerged, Perry burst into tears as he laid the child on the linen. Jennie collapsed back onto the pillow, breathing fast. "Perry, get a hold of yourself now. You need to cut the umbilical cord with the knife in one clean cut and tie it off with a piece of twine." Just as Perry was about to cut the cord, the curtain flung open and Mrs. Shenk burst through. "I'll take over from here, Mr. Duncan". Still sniffling, Perry handed the knife to Mrs. Shenk and backed out of the wagon. Sonny stood at the front of the wagon staring at Perry seated with his face in his hands. "Is Mrs. Jennie okay, Mr. Perry?" Before Perry could respond, Mrs. Shenk called out, "We need to have some clean hot water as soon as possible, Mr. Duncan." As Perry jumped off the wagon, he saw that Sonny had already started a fire and had placed a pail of water on the grate to heat. Walking up to Sonny, he grasped his shoulders and pulled the young man to himself in a strong embrace. "Sonny, thank you. How did you make it into Sheridan and back so quickly?" I took horse on a fast ride, Mr. Perry." Wiping the tears from his cheeks, Perry smiled and tousled Sonny's thick black hair. "You're a good man, Sonny."

Perry and Sonny stood above the fire watching for the water to start seething. As the first tiny bubbles sprang up in the water, Perry carried the pail of water to the wagon. "The water is warm now, Mrs. Shenk. Can I see Jennie now?" She replied sternly, "Not yet, Mr. Duncan. She'll be ready to see you in a bit. We have some details to finish in here." Perry backed away from the curtain and jumped off the wagon. The young Duncan boys stood intently tearful waiting for their father to give them the news on their mother. "Jesse sobbed, "We heard Ma crying, Pa. Is she going to be alright?"

"Your Ma is doing fine now, sons. Mrs. Shenk is taking care of her and the baby. We'll get to see her soon."

Inside the wagon, Mrs. Shenk gently washed the baby's face and body with the warm water. Muffled cries came from the wagon as she turned the child over on Jennie's stomach. Jennie whispered "Let me hold her, Mrs. Shenk" "I've almost finished here, Mrs. Duncan. This child is not a "she"! You have another son, Mrs. Duncan", she smiled as she laid the baby on Jennie's chest.

Jennie held her newborn to her face. Pressing her lips to his tiny head, tears filled her eyes and fell upon the child's face. Jennie pointed to the side box in the wagon and asked Mrs. Shenk to hand her the wrapped fabric she had purchased in the mercantile in Casper. Mrs. Shenk complied and handed the bundle to Jennie. Carefully unfolding the delicate fabric, she gently swaddled her infant.

Mrs. Shenk called down to Perry asking him to hand her satchel still strapped to the horse saddle.

Perry retrieved the satchel and carried it to Mrs. Shenk. "Can I see my wife now, Mrs. Shenk?" "We are almost finished in here, Mr. Duncan.

I just have one item that I must finish with your wife." Seated inside the clammy wagon next to Jennie, Mrs. Shenk removed a canvas measuring tape and a sheet of thin rice paper from the satchel. Placing the end of the measuring tape on the baby's heel, she stretched the tape to the tip of his head.

Writing on the moistened sheet, she noted that the child was born:

*September tenth, Nineteen Hundred One at five forty pm,
approximately six pounds and twenty one inches long.*

Scrolling her finger to the next line on the sheet, she asked, "Mrs. Duncan, what is this child's given name?"

Jennie's face, now sodden with tears, looked defiantly to Mrs. Shenk.

"This child is Sarah Jayne Houston Duncan."

B.J. KIRVEN

This story intertwines the events of Jennie Duncan's long envelopment of her husband and children in a life of seclusion and deception. Her insistence on moving from Colorado to homestead in Wyoming led to the unraveling of her web of deception in dangerous tribal territory. She steered her family to being exposed to the vulnerabilities of traveling alone on a primitive hazardous wagon trail.

Follow Jenny through the unforgiving environment of forsaken areas of Wyoming in a simple covered wagon with three young children and unpretentious husband. From bone chilling fear to passionate love, crushing loss and survival in desperate situations, the reader will come to respect this often wicked pioneer woman for her remarkable essence. Her life and the lives of her young family would be changed forever in an astonishing way from the events of the perilous trip across the Wyoming prairie.

Jennie Duncan's legacy endures in many ways today in Wyoming and Montana.

"See that you do not despise one of these little ones."

Matthew 18:1-5

48959337R00133

Made in the USA
San Bernardino, CA
09 May 2017